Brecht's Plays, Poetry and Prose
annotated and edited in hardback and paperback
by John Willett and Ralph Manheim
Methuen London publish all titles, Methuen New York only
those marked †

Collected Plays

Vol. 1	Baal; Drums in the Night; In the Jungle of Cities; The Life of
(hardback only)	Edward II of England; A Respectable Wedding; The Beggar; Driving Out a Devil; Lux in Tenebris; The Catch
Vol. 1i	Baal (*paperback only*)
Vol. 1ii	A Respectable Wedding and other one-act plays (*paperback only*)
Vol. 1iii	Drums in the Night (*paperback only*)
Vol. 1iv	In the Jungle of Cities (*paperback only*)
Vol. 2i	Man equals Man; The Elephant Calf
Vol. 2ii	The Threepenny Opera
Vol. 2iii	The Rise and Fall of the City of Mahagonny; The Seven Deadly Sins
*Vol. 3i	Saint Joan of the Stockyards
*Vol. 3ii	The Baden-Baden Cantata; The Flight over the Ocean; He Who Said Yes; He Who Said No; The Decision
*Vol. 4i	The Mother; The Exception and the Rule; The Horatii and the Curiatii
*Vol. 4ii	Round Heads and Pointed Heads
Vol. 4iii	Señora Carrar's Rifles; Fear and Misery of the Third Reich
Vol. 5i	Life of Galileo
Vol. 5ii	Mother Courage and her Children
*Vol. 5iii	The Trial of Lucullus; Dansen; What's the Price of Iron?
*Vol. 6i	The Good Person of Szechwan
Vol. 6ii	The Resistible Rise of Arturo Ui
*Vol. 6iii	Mr Puntila and his Man Matti
Vol. 7	The Visions of Simone Machard; Schweyk in the Second World War; The Caucasian Chalk Circle; The Duchess of Malfi
*Vol. 8i	The Days of the Commune
*Vol. 8ii	Turandot; Report from Herrenburg
*Vol. 8iii	Downfall of the Egoist Johann Fatzer; The Life of Confucius; The Breadshop; The Salzburg Dance of Death

Poetry
† Poems 1913—1956

Prose
  Brecht on Theatre
  Diaries 1920—1922
† Collected Short Stories 1921—1946
* Selected Essays

Also
† Happy End (by Brecht, Weill, Lane)

*in preparation

The following plays are also available (in paperback only) in unannotated editions:

The Caucasian Chalk Circle; The Days of the Commune; The Good Person of Szechwan; The Life of Galileo; The Measures Taken and other Lehrstücke; the Messingkauf Dialogues; Mr Puntila and his Man Matti; The Mother; Saint Joan of the Stockyards

BERTOLT BRECHT

The
Messingkauf
Dialogues

Translated by John Willett

METHUEN · LONDON

A METHUEN PAPERBACK
First published in Great Britain in 1965
Reprinted 1977 and 1978 by Eyre Methuen Ltd
Reprinted 1985 by Methuen London Ltd
Original work published under the title
DIALOGUE AUS DEM MESSINGKAUF
© *Suhrkamp Verlag Frankfurt am Main, 1963*
This translation © *Methuen & Co Ltd, 1965*
Printed in Great Britain by
Whitstable Litho Ltd., Whitstable, Kent

ISBN 0 413 38890 5

Contents

The First Night

The Second Night

5

CONTENTS

The Third Night

The Fourth Night

Appendices to the Messingkauf Theory

Notes

The German text is that of *Dialoge aus dem Messingkauf*, Suhrkamp-Verlag, Frankfurt, 1964, which is based on Volume 5 of Brecht's *Schriften zum Theater*; both being edited by Werner Hecht. The 'Practice Scenes for Actors' appended there have been omitted in the present version, which, however, retains the '*Appendices to the "Messingkauf" Theory*'.

Footnotes not by Brecht are marked (Ed.) or (Trans.), according as to whether they are by the editor or the translator.

Der Messingkauf means literally 'the purchase of brass'. Its significance will appear from page 15.

Characters of the Messingkauf

THE PHILOSOPHER wishes to apply the theatre ruthlessly to his own ends. It must furnish accurate images of incidents between people, and allow the spectator to adopt a standpoint.

THE ACTOR wishes to express himself. He wants to be admired. Story and characters serve his purpose.

THE ACTRESS wishes the theatre to inculcate social lessons. She is interested in politics.

THE DRAMATURG* puts himself at the Philosopher's disposal, and promises to apply his knowledge and abilities to the conversion of the theatre into the thaëter of the Philosopher. He hopes the theatre will get a new lease of life.

THE ELECTRICIAN represents the new audience. He is a worker and dissatisfied with the world.

* (Trans.) A *Dramaturg* is a play-reader and literary odd-job man, and is part of the staff of most German-language theatres. He may occasionally direct a play. Often he is a playwright himself, as Brecht was when he was one.

The First Night

A stage on which a Stagehand is slowly dismantling the set. An Actor, a Dramaturg and a Philosopher are sitting on chairs or set-pieces. The Dramaturg reaches for a small basket put there by the Stagehand, and takes out bottles which he then uncorks. The Actor pours the wine into glasses and hands it round.

THE ACTOR: All this dust makes it thirsty work sitting on a stage. You'd better take a good swig.

THE DRAMATURG *indicating the Stagehand*: Perhaps we should ask our friend here not to dismantle the set too quickly, so as to keep the dust down.

THE STAGEHAND: I won't hurry. It's got to be done tonight though; they're rehearsing tomorrow.

THE DRAMATURG: I hope it's all right for you here. We could have used my office, but it's colder there. The cash customers get better treatment, and anyway it'd mean sitting under the reproachful eyes of all those scripts I ought to have read. Besides, you as a philosopher rather like seeing behind the scenes, and you as an actor mayn't have much of a public, but at least you can play to its seats. We can talk about the theatre and feel as if we were holding a discussion in front of an audience, as if we were performing a little play. And now and again that will allow us to stage a small experiment or two to help clarify matters. So let's make a start; and why not by asking our friend the philosopher what interests him about the theatre in the first place?

THE PHILOSOPHER: What interests me about your theatre is the fact that you apply your art and your whole apparatus to imitating incidents that take place between people, with the result that one feels one is in the presence of real life. As I'm interested in the way people live together I'm interested in your imitation of it too.

THE DRAMATURG: I get it. You want to find out about the world. We show what takes place there.

THE PHILOSOPHER: You haven't got it entirely, I think. Your remark lacks a certain uneasiness.

THE DRAMATURG: What am I supposed to be uneasy about? You say you're interested in the theatre because we show what goes on in the world; and that's just what we do.

THE PHILOSOPHER: I said you dealt in imitations, and that they interested me in so far as they corresponded to what's imitated, because it's that that interests me most, i.e. people's living together. In saying that, I was expecting you to look dubiously at me and wonder whether anybody who approaches it in such a way can possibly be a good theatregoer.

THE DRAMATURG: Why should that stop you from being a good theatregoer? We've given up having gods and witches and ghosts and animals on the stage. During the past few decades the theatre has done all it could to reflect real life. It has made enormous sacrifices in its efforts to help solve social problems. It has shown how wrong it is that women should be treated as mere playthings, or that the individual's business conflicts should be carried into the home, turning marriages into battle-fields, or that the money for the educational refinement of rich men's children should come from other parents selling their children into immorality, and much more. And it has paid for such services to society by sacrificing virtually every element of poetry. It hasn't allowed itself to create a single major story fit to be compared with the classics.

THE ACTOR: Or a single major character.

THE DRAMATURG: What we do show, however, is banks, hospitals, oilfields, battlefields, slums, millionaires' villas, cornfields, stock exchanges, the Vatican, arbours, country houses, factories, conference tables – in fact, the whole of reality as we know it. You get murders being committed, contracts being signed, divorces being made absolute, heroic deeds being performed, wars being decided on; you get dying, breeding, buying, slandering and black marketeering. In short every possible facet of human social life is enacted. We look for anything that is powerful and effective, we'll consider any new idea, we've long ago scrapped all rules of aesthetics. Plays can have five acts or fifty; you can have five separate places shown on the stage at once; the ending can be happy or unhappy; we've had plays where the audience could choose whatever ending it liked. On top of that our acting can be naturalistic one night and stylized the next. Our actors can speak blank verse or gutter language, both equally well. Our musical comedies quite often turn out to be tragic, our tragedies include songs. One night the stage can show a house that is realistic down to the last detail, to the last stovepipe; the next night a wheat market can be represented by a few coloured poles. Our clowns make the audience shed tears, our tragedies reduce it to helpless laughter. With us, in other words, everything is possible. Should I add 'alas'?

THE ACTOR: That seems to me a rather pessimistic way of putting it. You make it sound as if we weren't serious any more. Let me tell you, we aren't just featherbrained slapstick merchants. We're a hardworking, highly disciplined lot of people trying to do their best; we have to be, because there's so much competition.

THE DRAMATURG: Our representations of real life were good enough to serve as models. The audience could study the subtlest inner moods and feelings. Our family interiors were exact replicas. Particular companies might spend ten years as an ensemble, so that one got representations, say, of a landowner's family where each movement of each actor was authentic and one could almost smell the scent of the rose garden. It used to amaze me how playwrights managed every time to discover some new inner sentiment for their characters just when we were beginning to think we knew them all. No, we stuck at nothing, and no trouble was too much for us.

THE PHILOSOPHER: So what you're mainly concerned with is imitating incidents between people?

THE DRAMATURG: We couldn't exercise our art if we didn't. The only thing you might say is that our imitations are bad ones. In that case you would be arguing that we are bad artists, because our art lies in giving our imitations the hall-mark of reality.

THE PHILOSOPHER: I'm not accusing you of that at all. I want to talk about your art where it's well done, not badly. And when well done it does give the hall-mark of reality to imitation.

THE ACTOR: I can say without undue boasting, I hope, that I could portray any action you might care to think of, however far-fetched you cared to make it, in such a way that you'd believe it without question. I'll show you the Emperor Napoleon chewing tintacks if you like, and I bet you'll find it absolutely natural.

THE PHILOSOPHER: Quite.

THE DRAMATURG: Excuse me, but you're sidetracking us. There's no need to overdo it.

THE ACTOR: What do you mean, sidetracking? I'm talking about the art of acting.

THE PHILOSOPHER: I wouldn't call that sidetracking either. There's an account of some well-known exercises for actors, designed to encourage natural acting, which includes the following drill: the actor places a cap on the floor and behaves as if it were a rat. This is supposed to teach him the art of inspiring belief.

THE ACTOR: A first-rate exercise. If we didn't master this art of inspiring belief how on earth could we get the spectator to look at a few flaps of canvas or even a sign with some writing on it and believe it's the scene of the battle of Actium he's seeing, or at a mask and a few antiquated articles of clothing and believe it's Hamlet? The greater our art, the less aids we need from reality in order to construct a slice of life. It's quite true that we imitate events from real life, but there's more to it than that. To hell with the incidents. What counts is our reason for imitating them.

THE PHILOSOPHER: Well, what is the reason?

THE ACTOR: Because we want to fill people with sensations and passions, to take them out of their everyday life and its events. The events are simply the framework on which we deploy our art, the springboard for us to take off from.

THE PHILOSOPHER: Exactly.

THE DRAMATURG: I don't like that 'exactly' one little bit. You wouldn't be all that satisfied with those sensations and passions you're meant to be filled with, I suppose. You didn't mention that when you were explaining why you come to our theatre.

THE PHILOSOPHER: True enough. Sorry. I'm drinking your health.

THE DRAMATURG: I'd sooner drink yours, if I may say so. Because what we were going to talk about was how *you* could get satisfaction from the theatre, not how we could.

THE ACTOR: I trust he's not going to say he minds our stirring up his sluggish soul. All right; he may be more interested in what we're imitating – yes, the events – than he is in us; but how are we going to imitate these events without calling on our sensations and passions? If we gave a frigid performance he'd just walk out. Anyway, one can't perform frigidly. Every event must stimulate us, so long as we're not entirely without feeling.

THE PHILOSOPHER: Oh, I've got nothing against feelings. I agree that feelings are necessary if representations, imitations of events from people's social life are to be possible; also that such imitations must stimulate feelings. The only thing that worries me is whether your feelings – more specifically your efforts to stimulate certain particular feelings – square with your imitations. You see, I'm afraid I must stick by my point that my main interest is in these events from real life. So let me stress once more that I feel I'm an intruder and an outsider in this building with all its mysterious practical bits of apparatus; like someone who has not come in to enjoy a sense of comfort and would have no hesitation in generating discomfort, as he has come with a quite particular interest whose particularity cannot be over-stressed. The particularity of my interest so strikes me that I can only compare myself with a man, say, who deals in scrap metal and goes up to a brass band to buy, not a trumpet, let's say, but simply brass. The trumpeter's trumpet is made of brass, but he'll hardly want to sell it as such, by its value as brass, as so many ounces of brass. All the same, that's how I ransack your theatre for events between people, such as you do more or less imitate even if your imitations are for a very different purpose than my satisfaction. To put it in a nutshell: I'm looking for a way of getting incidents between people imitated for certain purposes; I've heard that you supply such imitations; and now I hope to find out if they are the kind of imitations I can use.

THE DRAMATURG: Actually, I'm beginning to feel a little of the same discomfort as you prophesied for yourself. Imitations such as we 'supply' (as you so pithily put it) are naturally of a particular kind in so far as they are designed for a particular end. You'll find this point discussed in Aristotle's *Poetics*. He defines tragedy as an imitative representation of a self-contained morally serious action of such-and-such duration; in heightened speech whose different varieties are employed separately distributed among different parts; not narrated but performed by the persons taking part in it; stimulating pity and terror, and thereby bringing about the purging of those same moods. In other words, it's a matter of imitating your events from life, and the imitations are supposed to have specific effects on the soul. Since Aristotle wrote that, the theatre has gone through many transformations, but not on this point. One can only conclude that if it changed in this respect it would no longer be theatre.

THE PHILOSOPHER: You don't think it's feasible to distinguish your imitations from your purpose in making them?

THE DRAMATURG: Impossible.

THE PHILOSOPHER: But I need imitations of events from real life for my purposes. What can we do about it?

THE DRAMATURG: Imitations cut off from their purpose wouldn't be theatre, let me remind you.

THE PHILOSOPHER: That needn't particularly matter. We could call the result something different: 'thaëter', for instance. *All laugh.* It'd work like this: you'd just be artists whom I hired for an inartistic job. Finding myself unable to get hold of anybody else who was skilled in the exact imitation of active human beings, I would hire you for my purposes.

THE DRAMATURG: What are these mysterious purposes?

THE PHILOSOPHER *laughing*: Oh, I hardly like to tell you. You'll probably think they're terribly mundane and prosaic. I thought we might use your imitations for perfectly practical ends, simply in order to find out the best way to behave. You see, we could make them into something like physics (which deals with mechanical bodies) and so work out a technology.

THE DRAMATURG: So it's scientific purposes you're after! That's got nothing to do with art, you know.

THE PHILOSOPHER *hastily*: Of course. That's why I only called it 'thaëter'.

THE DRAMATURG: All right, let's have your ideas. There'll be something for us in them, too. It might be a roundabout way of getting a few hints about how to 'manufacture' good imitations. That's always important to us; we know by experience that our representations are much more effective when what we are representing isn't too unlikely. Nobody's going to sympathize with a jealous wife, for instance, if it's supposed that her husband is having an affair with her grandmother.

THE PHILOSOPHER: If I hire you, you can only hope to profit from such points as long as I don't lose from them. I think the first thing for me to do is find out exactly how you're used to working, so that I can see what needs changing in your methods if I am to get the right kind of imitations.

THE DRAMATURG: It may lead you to see that our imitations aren't all that unsuited to your purposes, even if we 'prepare' them in the old-fashioned way. In fact, I don't at all see why people shouldn't get practical lessons from our theatre, as well as everything else.

THE PHILOSOPHER: I ought to tell you that I have an insatiable curiosity about people; it's impossible for me to see and hear enough of them. The way they get along with each other, the way they develop friendships and enmities, sell onions, plan military campaigns, get married, make tweed suits, circulate forged bank-notes, dig potatoes, observe the heavenly bodies; the way they cheat, favour, teach, exploit, respect, mutilate and support one another; the way they hold meetings, form societies, conduct intrigues. I always want to know why they embark on their undertakings, and my aim is to distinguish certain laws that would allow me to make predictions. I ask myself how I ought to behave in order to get through and enjoy as much happiness as possible, and, of course, this depends on how everyone else behaves, which makes me very interested in that too, and specially in any possibility of influencing them.

THE DRAMATURG: Let's hope you can get your pound of flesh off us.

THE PHILOSOPHER: Yes and no. That's what I wanted to talk to you about, if I may say so. I'm not entirely happy here.

THE DRAMATURG: Why's that? Don't we show you enough?

THE PHILOSOPHER: Oh, quite enough. That's not the matter.

THE DRAMATURG: Perhaps you see things that don't seem to you to be represented right?

THE PHILOSOPHER: I also see things that do seem to me to be represented right. I think the trouble is that I find it impossible to distinguish right from wrong with you. Let me finish describing myself. You see, I've got another passion besides curiosity. That's disputatiousness. I like carefully weighing the pros and cons of everything I see and putting my own oar in. There's a certain pleasurable doubt in me. I finger people's acts and utterances just like a poor man fingering his loose change, and turn them over ten times. And I don't think you people here leave elbow-room for this doubt of mine; that's what it is.

THE ACTOR: Ha, a critic!

THE PHILOSOPHER: Hm. Have I touched a sore spot?

THE DRAMATURG: We don't mind intelligent criticism. We don't get enough.

THE ACTOR: It's all right. I understand: we'll always have to reckon with criticism of some sort.

THE PHILOSOPHER: You don't seem very taken with my enthusiasm. But let me assure you that I wasn't meaning to run down your art just now. I was only trying to explain the sense of unease that comes over me in your theatres and takes away a lot of the pleasure.

THE ACTOR: I hope you look inside yourself for the causes of that unease and don't only blame us.

THE PHILOSOPHER: Of course. I can give you encouraging reports too. We can clear the air a bit further, because I'm much less concerned with the way in which you represent things – that's to say, with whether your representation is right or wrong – than with the actual things you are imitating. Suppose you give a good imitation of a murder. My passion for criticism will then force me to subject the murder itself and all its details to tests of utility, elegance, originality and so on.

THE DRAMATURG: And you can't do that here?

THE PHILOSOPHER: No. You won't let me. It's something in the way you put on your imitations, even the best of them, and present them to me. Time was when I used to go to open-air performances and smoke during the play. As you know, a man smoking is in an attitude highly conducive to observation. He leans back, thinks his own thoughts, relaxes in his seat, enjoys everything from an assured position, is only half with it.

THE DRAMATURG: Did it help you see any better?

THE PHILOSOPHER: No, my cigar went out.

THE ACTOR: Bravo! A double round of applause! For the actor who managed to carry you away, and for yourself, for not being such a cold fish!

THE PHILOSOPHER: Stop. I must protest. It didn't turn out as I expected. The experiment was a failure.

THE ACTOR: Just as well, my dear man, just as well.

THE PHILOSOPHER: I wasn't satisfied.

THE ACTOR: Shall I tell you how you could have been? If those chaps on the stage had been a bunch of incompetents who couldn't act.

THE PHILOSOPHER: I'm rather afraid you may be right.

THE DRAMATURG: What do you mean, afraid?

THE PHILOSOPHER: Well, isn't it frightening if I get harder to satisfy the better you act? It sounds like a hopeless situation.

THE DRAMATURG to the Actor: Stop patting him on the shoulder in that condescending way. It can make people contradict even the most sensible remarks.

THE PHILOSOPHER: Yes, you are rather a dictatorial character, aren't you? It feels as if you're always dictating when you are on stage, too. I'm supposed to do what you want, without getting a moment to consider whether I want the same as you.

THE DRAMATURG: There you are; now he feels you go patting him on the shoulder in the theatre too. What did I tell you?

THE PHILOSOPHER: There could be something in this, don't you think? Look: a member of the audience says he feels he's being patted on the shoulder. Being seen through, understood better than he understands himself, caught out in secret desires, which are then satisfied. Isn't that rather gruesome?

THE ACTOR: Let's drop it. It's no good arguing if people can't keep their tempers. My hands are now in my pockets.

THE PHILOSOPHER: Who ever accused you of arguing, temper or no temper? You never argue on the stage, anyway. You provoke all sorts of passions, but a passion for argument – oh no. Indeed you don't even satisfy it when it's there.

THE DRAMATURG: Don't answer too quickly. He's talking very much to the point.

THE ACTOR: Yes. His point, though.

THE ACTOR: Frankly, I've begun to wonder if he's really a philosopher.

THE DRAMATURG: You ought to say why.

THE ACTOR: A philosopher thinks about things as they are. Here's art. So he thinks about it. It's this and that, and if he uses his loaf a bit perhaps he can explain why. If so he's a philosopher.

THE PHILOSOPHER: I entirely agree. There are philosophers like that. And art.

THE ACTOR: What art do you mean?

THE PHILOSOPHER: Art that is this and that, and that's all.

THE ACTOR: Really? Is there some other kind of art, then? Art that isn't this and that, and isn't anything?

THE PHILOSOPHER: Take your time; I know you aren't used to taking your time, but just try.

THE ACTOR: Very well, I shall think. *He strikes an attitude.* Is that how you do it?

THE PHILOSOPHER *feeling his calf muscles*: No. Your muscles aren't relaxed enough. Let's start our thinking with a confession by me. I'm a philosopher who failed to use his loaf for your sort of philosophizing.

THE ACTOR: I offer my bosom for you to weep on.

THE PHILOSOPHER: I'd rather use the lady's, actually, and preferably to laugh on rather than weep. But to get back to the philosopher and the loaf: for a few centuries now, while some philosophers have been making inventions and discoveries in the realm of nature, others have begun wondering whether they had the loaf to master and refute certain statements by the ecclesiastical and other authorities. These statements were to the effect that everything is rightly and legitimately as it is. They wore themselves out in a critique of reason. They truly hadn't enough in the way of loaves or any other nourishment to tackle such powerful institutions as the Church. So I have been trying to think how the general supply of loaves can be increased.

THE ACTOR *laughing*: When I said 'use one's loaf' I meant, of course, for thinking, not for eating.

THE PHILOSOPHER: Oh, there's a profound connexion. The more loaves, the more loaves.

FRAGMENTS FROM THE FIRST NIGHT

Naturalism

THE PHILOSOPHER: Being just like you people – cold behind me, quarrels in front of me, never able to do what I can – I too retire into these opium dens. They provide me with a bit of oblivion and a slight interest in life. For at night I'm as utterly muddled as the town I live in.

THE ACTOR: What the devil have you got against opium? And if you're against it, how can you be for art? Even the most ignominious rotten wreck of a philistine becomes an artist of a sort as soon as he's drunk. His imagination gets to work. The walls collapse round his room or his favourite bar, specially the fourth wall we were talking about. He gets an audience and starts to perform. The porter throws away the loads that have been put on him; the subordinate can afford to ignore his superior; he's a subversive influence. He looks at the ten commandments and sees the joke; he pinches respectability's bottom. He philosophizes, he may even cry. Often his sense of justice gets inflated; he becomes furious at things that have nothing to do with him. As the victim of a system he is struck by the funny side. He is thus able to rise above it, as long as his legs will support him. In other words he becomes in all respects more human, and he produces.

THE DRAMATURG: Naturalistic performances gave one the *illusion* of being at a real place.

THE ACTOR: The audience looked into a room and thought it could smell the cherry orchards at the back of the house; it looked into a ship and seemed to feel the menace of the storm.

THE DRAMATURG: The fact that it's pure illusion emerged more clearly from naturalistic plays than from naturalistic performances. The playwrights in question were naturally just as ingenious in arranging the incidents as the non-naturalistic had been. They cut, combined, made characters meet at unlikely places, treated certain incidents more broadly and others more delicately, and so on. They stopped short as soon as there was any danger of spoiling one's illusion of dealing with reality.

THE ACTOR: What you're saying is that it's only a question of degree, of greater or lesser realism of representation. But it's just the degree that matters.

THE DRAMATURG: I'd say it was a question of the degree of one's illusion of dealing with reality, and I think it's more fruitful to sacrifice that illusion if one can change it for a representation that conveys more of actual reality.

THE ACTOR: You mean one that arranges, cuts, combines and pulls together without bothering about keeping up the illusion that we're dealing with real life?

THE PHILOSOPHER: Bacon says nature betrays herself more easily when manhandled by art than if you leave her to her own devices.

THE ACTOR: You realize that would mean one was dealing with the playwrights' views about nature and not with nature herself?

THE DRAMATURG: And you realize that the same applied to naturalistic plays? People were quite right to accuse the first naturalistic dramas (e.g. Hauptmann's, Ibsen's, Tolstoy's, Strindberg's) of being committed and tendentious.

THE DRAMATURG: Stanislavsky's main achievement was the works of his naturalistic period, though he incidentally made many experiments and also staged plays of the imagination. You have to talk about 'works' in his case, since following the Russian custom some of his productions have been running unchanged for more than thirty years, though they're now acted by entirely different casts. His naturalistic works, then, consist of elaborately detailed pictures of society. They're like those deep-dug soil samples which botanists put on the laboratory bench and examine. Action in these plays is reduced to a minimum, the whole of the time is devoted to depicting conditions; it's a matter of probing the inner life of individuals, though there's something for social scientists too. When Stanislavsky was at the height of his powers the Revolution broke out. They treated his theatre with the greatest respect. Twenty years after the Revolution it was like a museum where you could still study the way of life of social classes that had meantime vanished from the scene.

THE PHILOSOPHER: Why talk about social scientists? Were they the only people who could find out about the structure of society from him? Couldn't everybody?

THE DRAMATURG: I'd like to think so. He wasn't a scientist himself but an artist; one of the greatest of his age.

THE PHILOSOPHER: I see.

THE DRAMATURG: What he cared about was *naturalness*, and as a result everything in his theatre seemed far too natural for anyone to pause and go into it thoroughly. You don't normally examine your own home or your own eating habits, do you? None the less his works have historical value, let me tell you, even if he wasn't an historian; put that in your pipe and smoke it.

THE PHILOSOPHER: Historical value for historians, evidently.

THE DRAMATURG: He doesn't seem to interest you.

THE PHILOSOPHER: Oh, he may serve various social interests, but hardly that of social science, even if he can be made to contribute to it. The man who drops a pebble hasn't begun representing the law of gravity, you know; nor has the man who merely gives an exact description of its fall. One might say at a pinch that his remarks don't contradict the facts, but we need more than that, or at any rate I do. He's like nature itself simply saying 'ask me a question'. But he'll put immense obstacles in the questioner's way; just as nature does. And of course he won't be as good as nature. An image which has been mechanically drawn and made to serve many purposes cannot be anything but extremely imprecise. There are bound to be short cuts at the most instructive points; it's all bound to have been superficially done. Such images tend to be as embarrassing to the scientist as supposedly accurate flower paintings are. Magnifying-glasses and all other scientific instruments are equally useless in interpreting them. So much for their value as objects of scientific study. And let me add that the social scientist is likelier to get something out of the venting of opinions about social conditions than from the conditions themselves. But our main lesson is that this kind of art calls for scientists if its results are to take the direction that interests us.

THE DRAMATURG: All the same, certain social movements did have their roots in naturalism and its works. The audience was brought to see a whole lot of conditions that couldn't be tolerated – to feel that they were intolerable, I mean. Teaching in State schools, the restrictions preventing women from gaining their independence, hypocrisy in sexual matters – these things and many more were held up to criticism.

THE PHILOSOPHER: That sounds all right. The theatre was acting in the public interest, so it must have aroused the interest of the public.

THE DRAMATURG: Oddly enough the theatre didn't gain much by its self-sacrificing attitude. Certain abuses were eliminated, or, in most cases, dwarfed by worse ones. The subject-matter of the various plays was quickly exhausted, and often it could be shown that the theatre's representations were very superficial. Yet the theatre had sacrificed a lot: all its poetry, much of its ease. Its characters had become flat, its actions banal. Artistic and social decline went hand in hand. It was the less polemical and more descriptive of Stanislavsky's works that lasted best and had the most important artistic and (let's face it) social effects. But even they couldn't produce a single great character or a single story worth setting alongside the classics.

THE DRAMATURG: Naturalism didn't last very long. It was felt to be too uneventful for the politicians and too boring for the artists, and it turned into *Realism*. Realism is less naturalistic than naturalism, though naturalism is considered fully as realistic as realism. Realism never gives absolutely exact images of reality; that's to say, it doesn't go in for full-length reproduction of dialogues such as one actually hears; it bothers less about being mistaken for real life. It does try to go deeper into reality, though.

THE ACTOR: Between you and me, old chap, it's neither one thing nor the other. It's just unnatural naturalism. When anyone asks the critics to name realist masterpieces they always pick on naturalistic works. When you object to that they point out various arbitrary actions on the playwright's part, arrangements of 'reality', distortions in its 'reproduction' and so on. All that proves is that naturalism never gave an exact reproduction, but was merely pretending to exactness. Naturalism worked like this: you came to one of its performances, and you thought you were coming into a factory or a private garden. You saw (and also felt) just as much of reality as you saw (and felt) at the place in question, i.e. very little. You felt hidden tensions or you experienced sudden outbursts and so forth; in other words, you got nothing you wouldn't have got outside the theatre. The naturalists responded by inserting a so-called

Raisonneur, a character who spoke for the playwright's own opinions. This spokesman was a disguised chorus in naturalistic terms. Often the job was given to the hero. He saw further and felt deeper than the rest; that's to say he had been let into the playwright's secret plans. Any spectator who identified himself with him could feel how he 'mastered' situations. For the audience to identify itself with him he had to be a pretty schematic figure with as few individual characteristics as possible; this allowed him to 'cover' the highest possible proportion of the audience. So he had to be unrealistic. Plays with heroes of this kind were then called realistic, since such heroes told one something about reality, but in an unnaturalistic way.

THE PHILOSOPHER: But even supposing the audience can mentally or psychologically identify itself with such heroes, that doesn't put it in a position to master reality. If I identify myself with Napoleon I don't become him.

THE ACTOR: No, but you feel you're him.

THE DRAMATURG: Realism's for the scrap-heap too, I see.

THE PHILOSOPHER: That wasn't the question, was it? It's just that what you called realism doesn't seem to have been realism at all. The term 'realistic' was simply stuck on mere photographic reproductions of reality. By this definition naturalism was more realistic than what was called realism. Then a new element was introduced, that of mastering reality. This element led to the distintegration of naturalism, which had been the only basis for speaking of realism.

THE DRAMATURG: What went wrong?

THE PHILOSOPHER: You can't give a realistic picture of the character you are putting forward for identification (the hero) without making it impossible for the audience to identify itself with him. A realistic picture would mean that he had to change with events, which would make him too unreliable for such empathy; he would also have a very limited viewpoint, which would mean that the spectator who shared it would not see far enough.

THE DRAMATURG: In other words realism in the theatre is quite impossible.

THE PHILOSOPHER: I'm not saying that. The crux of the matter is that true realism has to do more than just make reality recognizable in the theatre. One has to be able to see through it too. One has to be able to see the laws that decide how the processes of life develop. These laws can't be spotted by the camera. Nor can they be spotted if the audience only borrows its heart from one of the characters involved.

Empathy

THE DRAMATURG: We had images. Naturalism's images resulted in criticism of the real world.

THE PHILOSOPHER: Feeble criticism.

THE DRAMATURG: What should we have done to make it stronger?

THE PHILOSOPHER: Those naturalistic images of yours were badly manufactured. The point of view you chose for your representations made genuine criticism impossible. People identified themselves with you and came to terms with the world. You were what you were; the world stayed as it was.

THE DRAMATURG: You can't say we're free from criticism. What flops, what notices!

THE PHILOSOPHER: You get criticized when your attempts at illusion fail. Just like a hypnotist who fails to bring off his hypnosis. The customer is criticizing an apple that is a lemon.

THE DRAMATURG: Oh, so you think he ought to criticize the lemon?

THE PHILOSOPHER: That's it. But the lemon's got to be a lemon.

THE DRAMATURG: So evidently you think we are performing barbaric war dances in honour of obscure and obscene religions, humbug, witchcraft, black masses?

THE ACTOR: Ibsen's Nora a black mass! The noble Antigone a barbaric war dance! Hamlet as humbug! I like that.

THE PHILOSOPHER: I must have got you wrong. Excuse me.

THE ACTOR: Very wrong indeed, my friend.

THE PHILOSOPHER: It must be because I took your speeches seriously and didn't realize those expressions were designed to pull my leg.

THE DRAMATURG: What's he after now? Which expressions?

THE PHILOSOPHER: That you are 'servants of the word', that your art amounts to a 'temple', that the audience has to be 'enthralled', that your productions are 'divine' and so on. I really imagined you must be keeping up some old religion.

THE DRAMATURG: They're only figures of speech. All they mean is that we take it seriously.

THE ACTOR: It's a kind of protection against the hubbub of the market-place, against cheap entertainment and all that.

THE PHILOSOPHER: Naturally I wouldn't have thought so if I hadn't actually seen 'enthralled' spectators in your theatres. Take tonight, for instance. When your Lear cursed his daughters a bald-headed man next me started snorting in such an extraordinary way that I wondered why he didn't wholly identify himself with your marvellous portrayal of madness, and start frothing at the mouth.

ACTRESS: He'd spent better evenings.

THE DRAMATURG: Mime started suddenly flourishing when playwrights constructed long, tranquil, soulful acts and you could get good opera-glasses from the manufacturers. Faces had a lot going on in them in those days; they became the mirror of the soul, which meant that they had to be held very still, so that the art of gesture dried up. It was all a matter of feelings; the body was just a container for the soul. This miming varied from night to night; you couldn't count on it; too many factors were involved. But gestures were even less organized; they mattered almost as little as in the case of orchestral musicians, who also execute all kinds of gestures as they play. Actors improvised, or at any rate tried to look as if they did. The Russian school developed exercises of its own, which were supposed to keep this sense of improvisation alive for the whole run of a play.

Not that that stopped people from noting certain turns of voice that came off on a particular occasion, and then justifying such turns or expressions by analyzing them, establishing their foundations and finding adjectives for them.

THE ACTOR: *Stanislavsky's* system sets out to give the stage the truth about reality.

THE PHILOSOPHER: So I gathered. The imitations I saw disappointed me.

THE ACTOR: They may have been bad ones.

THE PHILOSOPHER: Judge for yourself. I got the impression that it was more a matter of coating a sham with as much truth as possible.

THE ACTOR: How I loathe moralizing! Holding a mirror up to the great! As if they didn't admire their own looks in it! And as if, as a seventeenth-century physicist once put it, murderers, thieves and usurers murdered, stole and exploited only because they didn't realize how hideous it was. Then begging the oppressed for God's sake to start taking pity on themselves at last! That bitter draught of sweat and tears! The conveniences are too small, the workhouses have smoking chimneys, the ministers armaments shares and the clergymen sexual organs! I'm to take a stand against all that.

THE ACTRESS: For fifty nights I played a bank director's wife who's treated as a toy by her husband. I stood up for women being allowed to have professions too, and take part in the great rat-race, as hunter or hunted or both. At the end I was having to drink myself silly in order to be able to get such stuff past my lips.

THE ACTOR: There was another play where I got my chauffeur to lend me some trousers belonging to his unemployed brother, and made powerful speeches to the proletariat. Even in Henry the Fifth's armour* I never cut such a noble figure as in those trousers. I pointed out that all the wheels would stop turning if

---

* (Trans.) Brecht says 'im Kaftan Nathans des Weisen', referring to Lessing's play of that name.

the strong arm of the proletariat so willed it. It was at a moment when several million workers were going about without work. The wheels had stopped turning whether their strong arm willed it or not.

About Ignorance

From 'The Philosopher's speech about the ignorance of the majority' to the theatre people.

THE PHILOSOPHER: Allow me to tell you that the millions who are in danger and misery have no idea what the causes of that danger and misery may be. There is however a considerable minority that has quite a good idea. They in turn have taught a considerable number of people a considerable amount about their persecutors' methods. Not so many can see how the persecutors are to be got rid of. The persecutors can only be got rid of once enough people understand the causes of their dangers and miseries, and the way things really happen, and how to get rid of the persecutors. So it's a question of communicating this understanding to as large a number as possible. It isn't easy, however one chooses to set about it. Today I would like to discuss with you theatre people what you might be able to do.

THE PHILOSOPHER: All of us have very vague ideas about our actions; often we don't even know why we perform them. Science hasn't done much to combat prejudice on this point. People suggest such dubious motives as greed, ambition, anger, jealousy, cowardice and so on. If we look back at what has happened we think we can make certain calculations – estimates of our position at the time; projects, recognition of obstacles outside our own control. We didn't initiate these calculations, however; we just deduce them from our own actions at the time. We only dimly realize how dependent we are in every way in all our decisions. There's some sort of link-up between it all, we feel, but we don't know what. That's why most people take the price of bread, the lack of work, the declaration of war as if they were phenomena of nature: earthquakes or floods. Phenomena like this seem at first only to affect certain sections of humanity, or to affect the individual only in certain sectors of his habits. It's only much later that normal everyday life turns out to have become abnormal, in a way that affects us all. Something has been forgotten, something has gone wrong. Whole classes have their interests threatened without those classes ever having banded together to protect the interests which they have in common.

THE PHILOSOPHER: It's because people know so little about themselves that their knowledge of nature is so little use to them. They know why a stone falls in a particular way when you throw it, but why the man throwing it acts in that particular way is another matter. Thus they can cope with earthquakes, but not with their fellows. Every time I leave this island* I'm frightened that the boat may go down in a storm. But I'm not frightened so much of the sea really as of the people who might fish me out.

THE PHILOSOPHER: Because people nowadays live in huge communities on which they are wholly dependent, and because they always live in several communities at a time, they have to go about everything in a very roundabout way if they are ever to achieve anything. It may look as if their own decisions no longer played a part. The simple fact is that decisions have become more difficult.

THE PHILOSOPHER: The ancients thought that the object of tragedy was to arouse pity and terror. That could still be a desirable object, if pity were taken to mean pity for people and terror terror of people, and if the serious theatre accordingly tried to help eliminate those circumstances which make people fear and pity one another. For man's fate has become man himself.

* (Trans.) Brecht was presumably writing in Denmark, where he lived on one of the islands in Svendborg province.

THE PHILOSOPHER: The causes of a lot of tragedies lie outside the power of those who suffer them, so it seems.

THE DRAMATURG: So it seems?

THE PHILOSOPHER: Of course it only seems. Nothing human can possibly lie outside the powers of humanity, and such tragedies have human causes.

THE DRAMATURG: Even if that were true it wouldn't make any difference to the theatre. In the old days opponents used to confront one another on the stage. How's it to be done now? Somebody in Chicago can set a piece of machinery going that will destroy twelve people in Ireland, or maybe twelve thousand.

THE PHILOSOPHER: Then obviously that machinery must stretch as far as Ireland. The opponents can confront each other on the stage. There'll have to be a lot of technical changes, of course. A lot of human characteristics and passions that used to be important have ceased to matter. Others have taken their place. In any case, it's difficult to grasp very much without seeing beyond the individual to the major group conflicts.

THE PHILOSOPHER: The spectator isn't going to learn anything from having an incident just happen. It won't be understood simply by being seen.

THE DRAMATURG: You mean you want some kind of comment?

THE PHILOSOPHER: Or something in its portrayal that will be equivalent to comment: yes.

THE DRAMATURG: But what about learning from experience? You don't merely see things in the theatre; you share an experience. Is there any better way of learning?

THE PHILOSOPHER: We'll have to examine how people learn from experience without something equivalent to comment being incorporated in it. To start with, there are certain factors that prevent one from learning or becoming any cleverer from experience: for instance, when there are changes in the situation which take place too gradually; imperceptibly, as we say. Or if one's attention is distracted by other incidents happening at the same time. Or if one looks for causes in incidents that weren't the causes. Or if the person undergoing the experience has strong prejudices.

THE DRAMATURG: Surely there are experiences that would make him shed them?

THE PHILOSOPHER: Only if he has thought about it. Which may well bring him up against the obstacles I mentioned.

THE DRAMATURG: But don't you learn best by doing things yourself?

THE PHILOSOPHER: The kind of experience the theatre communicates isn't doing things yourself. And it'd be quite wrong to treat each experience as an experiment and try to get everything out of it that an experiment can yield. There's a vast difference between experiment and experience.

THE ACTOR: Do me a favour and don't give us an elaborate account of that difference. I can work it out for myself.

THE DRAMATURG: What about the transfer of direct sensations? For instance, when horror is aroused by horrible actions; or when one experiences horror, and one's own is strengthened by it?

THE PHILOSOPHER: We're not concerned with the fact that horror can be aroused by horrible incidents (in reproduction), except where this horror is strongly and infectiously expressed by a single individual, as happens in the theatre. In such cases there are some relevant lessons to be learned from modern physiology. You know Pavlov's experiments with dogs?

THE ACTOR: Let's have it; it sounds like something factual for once.

THE PHILOSOPHER: Of course, this is only an example. People aren't dogs, even if you treat them as such in the theatre, as you'll see. Pavlov threw meat to dogs and rang a bell at the same time. He measured the dogs' salivation on seeing the meat. Then he rang the bell without throwing any meat. His measurements showed that the dogs salivated just the same. They needed their saliva only to digest the meat, not to stand the bell ringing, but that didn't stop it coming into their mouths.

THE DRAMATURG: And what's the relevance of that?

THE PHILOSOPHER: Your audience is experiencing extremely

rich, complex, many-sided incidents, comparable with those of Pavlov's dogs: food plus bell-ringing. It might be that the desired reactions occurred in real-life situations which only shared certain features of those they have experienced with you, secondary features perhaps. In that case you'd be making them ill, just like Pavlov and the dogs. But of course this also happens in real life. People can experience real incidents and still go astray in this way; they have learnt the wrong lesson.

THE ACTRESS: Can our star have an example of that?

THE PHILOSOPHER: A lot of the lower middle classes react to a revolution as if it were simply a matter of getting their windows broken.

THE DRAMATURG: There's some truth in that. We once did a play about the Paris Commune, I remember. It portrayed a popular rising. To begin with we showed a shop being realistically smashed up in the course of it. Then we dropped that, as we didn't want to suggest that the Commune was hostile to small tradespeople. It made for an extremely unrealistic popular rising.

THE ACTOR: Not a very good example. All you needed to do was to show the shopkeeper's indifference to this 'secondary phenomenon'.

THE DRAMATURG: Nonsense. No real shopkeeper could have identified himself with him.

THE PHILOSOPHER: I'm afraid you're right. No: that sort of realistic touch will have to be cut.

What Interests the Philosopher about the Theatre

THE DRAMATURG: Diderot, who was a great revolutionary *dramaturg*, said the theatre ought to promote instruction and entertainment. It seems to me you want to eliminate the latter.

THE PHILOSOPHER: You've already eliminated the former. There's no longer anything instructive about your entertainments. Let's see if there's anything entertaining about my instruction.

THE PHILOSOPHER: Science scans every field for openings for experiments or the plastic representation of problems. They make models showing the movements of the planets; they make ingenious apparatuses to demonstrate how gases behave. They also experiment on people. But in this case the possibilities of demonstrating anything are extremely limited. So it struck me that your art might serve to imitate people for the purposes of such demonstration. Incidents from people's social life, demanding an explanation, could be imitated in such a way as to confront one with plastic representations whose lessons could be practically applied.

THE DRAMATURG: I take it that in staging these demonstrations one wouldn't just go about it aimlessly. There'd have to be some sense of direction; there'd have to be some criteria for the choice of incidents; one would at least need a hypothesis or two. What about that?

THE PHILOSOPHER: There is a science of people's social life: a great doctrine of cause and effect in this field. We can find our criteria there.

THE DRAMATURG: You mean the Marxist doctrine?

THE PHILOSOPHER: Yes. With one reservation, however. That doctrine deals above all with the behaviour of great masses of people. The laws it propounds apply to the movement of large human units, and although it has a good deal to say about the individual's position within those units this refers normally only to the relations between those masses and the individual. But in our demonstrations we'd be more concerned with the behaviour of individuals to one another. However, the main principles of the doctrine are also a great help in judging the individual: for instance the principle that people's consciousness depends on their social existence, taking it for granted at the same time that this social existence is continually developing and that their consciousness is accordingly changing all the time. A lot of well-worn principles are ruled out, such as 'it's all a matter of money', and 'history is made by great men', and 'two and two makes four'. Nor is there any question of another equally well-worn lot of principles replacing them.

The Philosopher's explanation of Marxism

THE PHILOSOPHER: It's important that you should understand the difference between Marxism, which recommends a particular way of looking at the world, and what is normally called a *Weltanschauung* or outlook. Marxism posits certain methods of looking, certain criteria. These lead it to make certain judgements of phenomena, certain predictions and suggestions for practical action. It teaches a combination of thinking and active intervention as a means of dealing with reality in so far as social intervention is able to deal with it. It is a doctrine that criticizes human action and expects in turn to be criticized by it. A true Weltanschauung, however, is a picture of the world, a hypothetical knowledge of the way in which things happen, mostly moulded in accordance with some ideal of harmony. You can learn about this distinction elsewhere, but it's important for you because when you imitate incidents you ought on no account to imagine that you are illustrating any of the numerous principles which the Marxists, as I have explained, put forward. You must examine it all and prove it all. The only way to clarify your incidents is by other incidents.

THE DRAMATURG: Give us an example.

THE PHILOSOPHER: Let's take the play *Wallenstein* by the German author Schiller. In it a general betrays his monarch. Instead of the sequence of incidents in the play proving that this betrayal necessarily leads to the traitor's moral and physical destruction, this is assumed from the first. The world can't exist on a basis of treachery, in Schiller's view. Though he does nothing to prove it. And he couldn't prove such a thing, because it would rule the world out. What he suggests is that it wouldn't be pleasant to live in a world like that, where treachery occurred. Not that he proves that either, of course.

THE DRAMATURG: How would a Marxist go about it?

THE PHILOSOPHER: He'd treat it as a historical case, with causes from that period and effects in that period.

THE DRAMATURG: And the moral problem?

THE PHILOSOPHER: He'd treat the moral problem as a historical one too. He would observe how a particular moral system worked and what function it served in a particular social order, and would fix the sequence of incidents so as to clarify it.

THE DRAMATURG: You mean he would criticize this fellow Wallenstein's moral opinions?

THE PHILOSOPHER: Yes.

THE DRAMATURG: From what point of view?

THE PHILOSOPHER: Not from that of his own moral principles.

THE DRAMATURG: All the same, I don't think it would be easy to learn this new method of representation either from the old plays, which indeed do only try to stimulate the emotions, by a few indications and reminiscences of reality, or from their naturalistic alternatives. We might perhaps take genuine court cases out of the law reports and rehearse them, or something of that sort. Or make our own adaptations of well-known novels. Or represent historical incidents as ordinary everyday ones, as the caricaturists do.

THE ACTOR: We actors depend entirely on the plays we get given. We don't just see one or two of your *incidents* and then imitate them on the stage. So we'll have to wait for new plays to come along that will allow the sort of performance you want.

THE PHILOSOPHER: That may mean you'll have to wait for ever. I suggest we shouldn't go on to discuss construction: at any rate not yet. Generally your playwrights take such incidents from real life as would arouse a reasonable amount of interest in real life, and tailor them in such a way as to make them effective on the stage. Even when they use their imagination, except in purely fantastic plays, they use it so that the incidents seem to have been taken from real life. All you need to do then is take the incidents themselves as seriously as possible, and the playwright's use of them as lightly as possible. There's no reason why you shouldn't leave out part of his interpretation, make fresh additions, and generally use plays as so much raw material. I'm assuming from the start that you will only pick plays whose incidents are of sufficient public interest.

THE ACTOR: What about the writer's message, the poet's sacred words; what about style, what about atmosphere?

THE PHILOSOPHER: Oh, I'd say the writer's intentions were only of public interest when they provoked the public's interest. His words can be treated as sacred if they are the right answer to the people's questions; style will depend on your own taste anyway; while the atmosphere needs to be clear, whether the writer makes it so or not. If he respects these interests and respects the truth, then you should follow him; if not, then amend him.

THE DRAMATURG: I'm not sure you're talking like a man of taste.

THE PHILOSOPHER: But like a man, I hope. There are times when you have to decide between being human and having good taste. Anyway, why go along with that rotten convention of only attributing good taste to people who know how to wear beautiful clothes, and not to the people who make them?

THE ACTOR: Don't you see that he's scared that we might mis-interpret some deliberate piece of impertinence as pure amia-bility? What do you imagine the painter Gauguin would have said if someone had looked at his Tahitian pictures only because of his interest in Tahiti, say because of the rubber business? He had every right to expect us to be interested in Gauguin, or at any rate in painting in general.

THE PHILOSOPHER: And suppose someone was interested in Tahiti?

THE ACTOR: There's plenty of other material for him apart from Gauguin's art.

THE PHILOSOPHER: Suppose there wasn't. Suppose the man who looked didn't want dry facts and statistics but a general impression; suppose for instance he wanted to know how people lived there. The rubber business isn't enough to stimulate a really deep, many-sided interest in a place like Tahiti, and as I told you I'm really – i.e. deeply and many-sidedly – interested in the object you are imitating.

THE DRAMATURG: Gauguin wouldn't be the right reporter though. He hasn't enough to offer for such purposes.

THE PHILOSOPHER: Possibly. He wasn't thinking of them. But could he give the right kind of report?

THE DRAMATURG: Maybe.

THE ACTOR: At the cost of sacrificing his artistic interests.

THE DRAMATURG: Oh, that wouldn't be essential. There's no reason why as an artist he shouldn't be interested in the kind of task our friend has set him. I seem to remember Holbein doing a job for Henry the Eighth that involved painting the portrait of a lady the king wanted to marry, but hadn't met.

THE ACTOR: I can see him at it. The courtiers grouped round him. *He acts.* 'Master, Master! Dost not observe her Highness's lips, so soft and swelling. . . .' and all that. 'Suffer not such voluptuous painting of your Highness's lips, your Highness. Consider the foggy airs of England!' 'And furthermore they are thin, thin, thin. Be not so foolhardy as to deceive the king.' 'It is the lady's nature that concerns the king; he is a man of much experience. Not will she attract him; but will she attract others?' ''Tis bad the posterior should be hid from him.' 'And far too lofty a brow.' 'Remember, Master, that these are high politics. For France's sake let the colour on your brush be greyer.'

THE ACTRESS: Does anybody know whether the marriage came off?

THE PHILOSOPHER: There's nothing about it in the art history books, anyway. The aesthetes who write them don't understand that kind of art. I think our friend here would have understood them, to judge from her question.

THE ACTRESS: Ah well, the lady's dead and her royal suitor has likewise turned to dust. But Holbein's portrait has just as much meaning today, even though it's no longer a matter of marriage and politics.

THE DRAMATURG: The picture could have taken on some special quality that we are still able to appreciate. It said so many important things about a woman, things that still interest us today.

THE PHILOSOPHER: We're getting away from the point, my friends. All that matters to me is that this portrait became a work of art. At any rate I think we'd all agree about that.

THE ARTIST: It may have been a job, but for Holbein it was just a motive for art.

THE DRAMATURG: But the fact that he was an artist was the king's motive for getting him to do the job he needed done.

THE ACTOR *getting up*: He's no theatregoer.

THE ACTRESS: What are you talking about?

THE ACTOR: He's got no feeling for art. He's out of place here. From art's point of view he's stunted, a poor wretch who was born lacking one particular organ: a feeling for art. Of course, he may be a perfectly respectable person in other ways. When it comes to finding out if it's raining or snowing, or if Smith is a good fellow and Brown's intelligent, and so on and so forth, you can rely on him, why not? He doesn't understand a thing about art, though, and what's more he doesn't want art; it makes him sick, it ought to be abolished. I've placed him now all right. He's the fat man in the stalls who has come to the theatre to meet a business colleague. As I'm bleeding to death up on the stage with my 'To be or not to be' I catch his fishy eye fixed on my wig; as the wood advances towards* Dunsinane against me I see him wondering what it's made of. The highest he can reach is the circus, I'm sure. A two-headed calf: that's the sort of thing his imagination's fired by. A leap from fifteen feet: that's the epitome of art for him. There's something really difficult for you. Something you can't do yourself, that's what art is, isn't it?

THE PHILOSOPHER: As you are so very insistent, let me admit that I do indeed find a fifteen-foot leap interesting. Is that wrong? But I'm interested in calves with only one head, too.

THE ACTOR: Oh yes, if it's the real thing, a genuine calf, no imitations, eh? The calf in person, related to its background and with particular reference to its nourishment. You've come to the wrong place, sir.

---

* (Trans.) Brecht says '*from* Dunsinane', but Shakespeare says otherwise.

THE PHILOSOPHER: But I assure you I've seen you yourself
performing the equivalent of such leaps, and very interesting I
found it. You too can do things I can't do myself. In my view
I've got just as much feeling for art as the majority of mankind:
a thing I have often noted, sometimes with satisfaction, sometimes with concern.

THE ACTOR: You're trying to talk yourself out of it. Talk, talk,
talk! I can tell you exactly what you mean by art. It's the art of
making copies, copies of what you choose to call reality. Sir,
art *is* reality. Art is so far above ordinary reality that it'd be
fairer to call reality a copy of art. A very incompetent one, at
that.

THE ACTRESS: Aren't you and art trying to leap rather too high?

The Second Night

The Philosopher's Speech about our Period

THE PHILOSOPHER: Remember that we have met together in a dark period, when men's behaviour to one another is particularly horrible and the deadly activities of certain groups of people are shrouded in almost impenetrable darkness, so that much thought and much organization is needed if behaviour of a social kind is to be dragged into the light. The vast oppression and exploitation of one man by another, the warlike slaughterings and peaceable degradations of every sort throughout our planet have come to seem pretty well natural to us. Many of us, for instance, find the exploitation that takes place between men just as natural as that by which we master nature: men being treated like the soil or like cattle. Countless people approach great wars like earthquakes, as if instead of human beings natural forces lay behind them against which the human race is powerless. Perhaps what seems most natural of all to us is the way we earn our living: the way one man sells another a cake of soap, a loaf of bread, or the strength of his body. We imagine that it's simply a free exchange of commodities, but you only have to look closely to see just what the fearful experiences of our daily life go to prove: that such exchanges don't merely take place between people but are managed by specific people. The more we can squeeze out of nature by inventions and discoveries and improved organization of labour, the more uncertain our existence seems to be. It's not we who lord it over things, it seems, but things which lord it over us. But that's only because some people make use of things in order to lord it over others. We shall only be freed from the forces of nature when we are free of human force. Our knowledge of nature must be supplemented with a knowledge of human society if we are to use our knowledge of nature in a human way.

The Actor's Speech about how to Portray a Little Nazi

THE ACTOR: In accordance with our rule-of-thumb methods I didn't try to make the character interesting by making him unfathomable; I tried instead to create interest in his fathomability. As it was my job to provide a portrait of this man which would make it easier for society as represented by our own audience to deal with him I obviously had to portray him as a basically alterable personality, and for this the new methods of acting we've been discussing were very handy. I had to make it possible to gain insights into him of such a kind that as many as possible of the interventions which society had made at one time or another became visible. I had furthermore to give some idea of the extent to which he would be alterable under given circumstances, since society isn't always in a position to mobilize enough forces to alter each of its members so that he immediately becomes useful; quite often the best it can do is to render a member harmless. But whatever happened I couldn't create anything like a 'born Nazi'. What I had in front of me was something contradictory, an atom, as it were, of the people that hated the people: the little Nazi, who's one of the mass yet against the mass's interests, a swine when among Nazis perhaps or a bigger swine when among the Nazis, yet at the same time an ordinary person, i.e. a human being.* Just because he was one of the mass he enjoyed a certain anonymity, sharing the characteristics of a group alongside a lot that was individual. It's a family like any other, and at the same time it's not a family like any other. I had to make him take every step as if there was an explanation

---

* The whole is swinish, but the whole is more than the sum of its parts. The older ones were in it for what they could get, but there was a kind of half-stifled social idealism about the younger.

for it, and at the same time to have an inkling of some different step for which there would have been an explanation too. People ought never to be treated as if they can only act one way; they could act differently. Our houses have fallen about our ears; they could be standing.

FRAGMENTS FROM THE SECOND NIGHT

Science*

THE PHILOSOPHER: People who know nothing about either science or art imagine that those are two vastly different things that they know nothing about. They fancy they're doing science a favour if they allow it to be unimaginative, and are promoting art if they stop people expecting it to be intelligent. A man's talents may lie in a particular direction, but he won't become any more talented in that direction by being untalented in all others. Knowledge is as much a part of humanity as art is, even if the decrepitude of our social life means that it often has to get along without either for long periods. Nobody is entirely without knowledge, so nobody is entirely without art.

THE ACTOR: Everything'll soon be utterly *practical*. Subjects like State of the Public Water Supply in Sink Street, and Tenants are Requested Not to Play the Wireless after Ten o'clock. Stripped of all the essentials.

THE ACTRESS: That will be instead of 'Young Man's World-

* (Trans.) The German word *Wissenschaft* means science in its original sense of 'knowledge', almost 'scholarship'. The sciences in our sense are *die Naturwissenschaften*. Any scholarly discipline can be a *Wissenschaft*: history, literary studies (*Literaturwissenschaft*), the history of the theatre (*Theaterwissenschaft*) and so on. The term is always translated as 'science', but the distinction should be borne in mind.

weariness on account of Sexual Inhibitions' or 'Mother Hears Only Son is a Forger', with full details.

THE DRAMATURG: As far as I can see, nothing our friend has said so far suggests that one of the four themes you've mentioned mightn't occur in his *thaëter*. As for the themes' degree of importance, society as represented by the spectators is fully capable of deciding that. *All* interests come together there.

THE PHILOSOPHER: I think our friend the actor's objections are directed at the narrowness of our supposedly pure practical men. He's afraid we might adopt their smart-alec methods of 'getting to grips' with all one's problems, solving everything in a jiffy and shelving anything they find beyond them. But why should we?

THE DRAMATURG: You have to admit that by hiring art as a mere means we've pretty well written it off. And it's characteristic of art to raise questions without knowing the answer, to convey oppression without identifying the means used, and so on.

THE PHILOSOPHER: It's characteristic of science too, my friends.

THE DRAMATURG: Possibly, but all the same science is far more practical. If it puts forward something it doesn't understand, it doesn't abdicate from understanding. Art makes a fetish of incomprehensibility. It gets intoxicated by the 'fact' that there are things beyond the human reason, outside our power. It teams up with fate.

THE PHILOSOPHER: So did science in earlier times, and in some fields it still does. Nature wasn't always mastered immediately; humanity didn't always immediately reconcile itself to its fate.

THE ACTOR: Theatre or thaëter, we're still dealing with human nature. That's what determines humanity's fate.

THE PHILOSOPHER: The same applies to this section of nature as applies to nature as a whole. We've agreed that we'll speak as little as possible about art, its special laws, limitations, advantages, obligations, etc. We've downgraded it to a mere means, trodden it under foot, raped it and enslaved it and deprived it of its rights. We feel we're no longer obliged to express dark premonitions, bits of unconscious knowledge, unmanageable feelings and so on. On the other hand our new task demands that we put forward whatever takes place between people, fully and completely, complete with all contradictions, in a state that can or cannot be resolved. Nothing is irrelevant to society and its affairs. The elements that are clearly defined and can be mastered must be presented in relation to those that are unclear and cannot; these too have a place in our thaëter.

THE DRAMATURG: I see that what you miss is the touch of something special, distinctive, striking. But we don't rule that out. We don't act as if *all* scientists got angry at such a suggestion. We can portray this kind or that kind.

THE PHILOSOPHER: And how do you do that?

THE ACTOR: If he's the kind that gets angry I make him that way from the start. His outburst must come logically, fit in with his other remarks, emerge from the general course of it all. *My* man gets angry; nobody's going to fail to understand that.

THE PHILOSOPHER: In other words things that happen, happen.

THE DRAMATURG: You've got a nasty way of saying that, as if we only supplied what the customers wanted, only said what they liked. A better way of putting it would be 'what has to come comes'.

THE PHILOSOPHER: Let's suppose someone gets angry at some suggestion which he feels is an insult to his dignity. That a servant should betray his master, for instance, or a scientist his science. To start with the actor will produce something general, like an illustration of the gest:* *What do they take me for?* This is a gest that almost anyone can understand; almost anyone can imagine a situation where he gets angry as he thinks: *What do they take me for?* Of course, the actor will alter the basic gest to fit the character: give the servant what is the servant's and the scientist what is the scientist's. There will be some indication of period, at least by means of the costumes.

* (Trans.) Brecht's word *Gestus* is best translated by this obsolete English word meaning 'bearing', 'carriage', 'mien'. *Gestus* is not simply gesture, but a combination of gesture and attitude. A play, a person, a sentence can all have a *Gestus*.

What will emerge? That such a suggestion enrages me and enrages you; that it enrages the servant and the scientist; that it always has enraged people and always will.

THE ACTOR: Exactly. Because we are acting in the present, and out of the passions of the past we have to choose those that still exist, and we are acting simultaneously to servants and to scientists.

THE PHILOSOPHER: Yes, and that means that you have to be careful that your outburst of anger doesn't meet with astonishment. Things that happen must be able to happen in the sense that what goes on must be able to go right through.

THE PHILOSOPHER: It's also important that the actor should show that he knows what it's like to be observed, because that can teach the spectator to behave in everyday life like a man under observation. This is where the actor is a model to be imitated. The individual gets immense advantages from being aware of being observed, and society too can only profit from it.

THE PHILOSOPHER: If we observe sorrow on the stage and at the same time identify ourselves with it, then this simultaneous observing is a part of our observation. We are sorrowful, but at the same time we are people observing a sorrow – our own – almost as if it were detached from us, in other words like people who aren't sorrowful, because nobody else could observe it so detachedly. In this way we aren't wholly dissolved in sorrow; something solid still remains in us. Sorrow is hostile to thought; it stifles it; and thought is hostile to sorrow.

THE ACTRESS: It can be a pleasure to cry.

THE PHILOSOPHER: Crying doesn't express sorrow so much as relief. But lamenting by means of sounds, or better still words, is a vast liberation, because it means that the sufferer is beginning to produce something. He's already mixing his sorrow with an account of the blows he has received; he's already making something out of the utterly devastating. Observation has set in.

THE DRAMATURG: The closest thing to what you want would be the explorer's way of representing the customs and habits of savage people. He uses the most dispassionate tone to describe the most passionate war dances. Though I admit that it makes a difference if the representation is physical. Allowing that certain movements are very difficult to make without undergoing certain emotions, and allowing also that certain movements provoke certain emotions, how is the actor to portray signs of passion, such as surely have to be reported too?

THE PHILOSOPHER: Anyone who has observed with astonishment the eating habits, the judicial processes, the love life of savage peoples will also be able to observe our own eating customs, judicial processes and love life with astonishment. Miserable philistines will always find the same motive forces in history, their own. And those only so far as they are aware of them, which is not very far. Man with a capital M drinks coffee every afternoon, is jealous of his wife, wants to get on in the world, and only more or less manages to: more often less. 'People don't change much,' he says, and if he himself is less agreeable to his wife than he was twenty years ago it's just that men always have been less agreeable to their wives at forty-five than at twenty-five. 'Love is timeless,' he says, and would sooner have no idea of the term's original meaning and the practices covered by it. He changes just as much as a pebble in a river bed, knocking against the other pebbles. And like a pebble he moves forward. As he has no object in life, he could really achieve anything 'given the right circumstances': conquer the world like *Caesar*, for instance. Anything can happen to him; he's at home in any disaster. He has been rewarded with ingratitude like *Lear*, been enraged like *Richard III*. He has given up everything for his wife, like *Antony* did for Cleopatra, and has nagged her more or less as *Othello* did his. He is as hesitant as *Hamlet* to right a wrong by bloodshed; his friends are like *Timon's*. He is exactly like everybody; everybody is like him. Differences don't matter; it's all one to him. In all men he can see only Man, the singular of the plural word 'people'. And so his intellectual poverty infects everything with which he comes into intellectual touch.

THE PHILOSOPHER: We observe our social environment too as if it were part of nature, almost like landscape. Money that produces interest we regard like a pear tree that produces pears. Wars, because they have similar effects to earthquakes and appear equally unavoidable, we regard as if they were earthquakes. Regarding something like marriage we just murmur: 'It's what's natural.' It amazes us to hear that in other parts of the world, or in our own at other periods, people have regarded other relationships between man and woman as the natural ones.

THE PHILOSOPHER: What's bad isn't that one should fail to see every link of the chain, but that one should miss the chain itself. We were complaining how difficult it was to make opponents confront each other on a single stage. It's true that new techniques can do a good deal to overcome this, but the main thing is that it shouldn't seem as if there were no opponents at all. Quite often a *dramaturg* may fail to see the opponent or fail to make him visible, and will therefore try to bring out some other element which seems more obvious and makes some kind of basis for the incident. The hero's own character, handicaps applying specifically to him, and so on. And he then develops a smooth sequence of motivations, whereas in real life the fact that the motive causes lie outside leads necessarily to twists and turns which cannot be explained in terms of the material already provided. Against that, when the opponents are brought on stage together it can very often give a misleading picture, for instance when their opposition is made to seem natural and necessary. There's a play called *The Weavers* by a playwright who, when a decrepit old man, came to play an ignominious part under the housepainter,* and in it the factory-owner was made to seem merely an avaricious character, leading one to believe that the miserable state of the weavers couldn't be cured

* (Trans.) Hitler.

without eliminating this avarice. The mutual hostility of the man who had the capital and the people who did the work seemed perfectly natural, as natural as that of lion and lamb.

THE PHILOSOPHER: The physicists say that they have suddenly come to suspect, in the course of their observations of the very smallest particles of matter, that the process of observation has altered what is being observed. The motions which they observe through the microscope are complicated by motions which the microscope causes. At the same time the instruments are being altered, apparently by the objects they are focused on. If that's what happens when instruments do the observing, what happens when men do?

THE DRAMATURG: You allot a very important place to reason. It's as if you wouldn't admit anything that hadn't first been filtered through the brain. I don't agree with the view that artists have less reasoning power than other people (though it's arguable), but they have more faculties to work with than just their reason. If you're only prepared to pass what they have registered and docketed in their brains not much is going to reach the stage.

THE PHILOSOPHER: There's something in what you say. People do a lot that is reasonable, but has never been subjected to their reason; it would be wrong for us to renounce that. There's the question of instinct and also all those types of action which represent an indecipherable tangle of highly varied and contradictory efforts and motives. I see no risk in planting a great ladleful of them on the stage. The one thing that matters is that they should be presented in such a way that they can be weighed up, and that there should be something complex and instinctive about the weighing. There are other ways of planting things, as you know.

THE DRAMATURG: We might say a few words about the moral aspect. There are also labels like 'good' and 'bad'. Is everything to be labelled like that?

THE PHILOSOPHER: What a ghastly idea! It would be the height of folly. Of course, an artist has got to have some liking for human beings. This enjoyment of humanity can lead him to appreciate the bad impulses, too; that is to say those impulses which are rightly or wrongly dubbed harmful to society. I'd say it was enough that you should stand for society's point of view in the broadest possible sense, and not just for that of some particular temporary social form. You must not persecute the individual, who is persecuted so often. You must keep the whole in view and see that the audience keeps it in view likewise.

Removal of Illusion and Empathy

THE DRAMATURG: What about the fourth wall?

THE PHILOSOPHER: What's that?

THE DRAMATURG: Plays are usually acted as if the stage had four walls, not three; the fourth being where the audience is sitting. The impression given and maintained is that what happens on the stage is a genuine incident from real life, which of course doesn't have an audience. Acting with a fourth wall, in other words, means acting as if there wasn't an audience.

THE ACTOR: You get the idea? The audience sees quite intimate episodes without itself being seen. It's just like somebody looking through a keyhole and seeing a scene involving people who've no idea they are not alone. Actually, of course, we arrange it all so that everyone gets a good view. Only we conceal the fact that it's been arranged.

THE PHILOSOPHER: Ah yes, then the audience is tacitly assuming that it's not in a theatre at all, since nobody seems to take any notice of it. It has an illusion of sitting in front of a keyhole. That being so it ought not to applaud till it starts queuing for its hats and coats.

THE ACTOR: But its applause confirms the very fact that the actors have managed to perform as if it weren't there.

THE PHILOSOPHER: Do you think we need this elaborate secret understanding between the actors and yourself?

THE WORKER: I don't need it. But perhaps the actors do.

THE ACTOR: For realistic acting it's considered essential.

THE WORKER: I'm for realistic acting.

THE PHILOSOPHER: But it's also a reality that you are sitting in a theatre, and not with your eye glued to a keyhole. How can it be realistic to try and gloss that over? We want to demolish the fourth wall: I herewith announce our joint operation. In future please don't be bashful; just show us that you've arranged everything in the way best calculated to help us understand.

THE ACTOR: That's official, is it, that from now on we can look down at you and even talk to you?

THE PHILOSOPHER: Of course. Any time it furthers the demonstration.

THE ACTOR *mutters*: So its back to asides, to 'Honoured Sirs, behold before you King Herod', and to the girls showing off their legs to the officers in the boxes. . . .

THE PHILOSOPHER *mutters*: The hardest advance of all: backwards to common sense.

THE ACTOR *explodes*: Sir, we all know the theatre has gone downhill in many ways. But so far it has at least respected the forms. It never addressed the audience directly, for instance. However corrupt and feebleminded it may have become, at any rate it didn't make itself cheap. You could only associate with it by going through the proper channels. Up to now, sir, we've not been performing for any old Tom, Dick and Harry who could afford the price of a ticket, but for the sake of art.

THE WORKER: Who does he mean by Tom, Dick and Harry?

THE PHILOSOPHER: Us.

THE ACTOR: Art, sir. And you people just happen to be present. Perhaps you wouldn't mind trying the building next door, where you'll find establishments where the girls show you their bottoms as required.

THE PHILOSOPHER: And in yours the girls show their bottoms exclusively to their fellow actors, with whom it's perfectly respectable to identify oneself; is that it?

THE DRAMATURG: Watch it, gentlemen.

THE WORKER: *He's* the one brought the bottoms into the argument.

THE PHILOSOPHER: Meanwhile all they're really doing is showing us their souls.

THE ACTOR: And that's nothing to be ashamed of, you mean? And what d'you mean by 'all'?

THE DRAMATURG: It's a pity you always let him get a rise out of you. Now that you've reacted with philosophic anger, can't you act with philosophic serenity?

THE PHILOSOPHER: Our critical attitude springs from the fact that we have developed great faith in humanity's powers of work and invention, and have grown sceptical of the idea that everything must remain as it is, even if it is as rotten as our State institutions. There may once have been a time when force and oppression compelled men to produce great works, when the possibility of exploiting people set minds moving towards plans that were of some value to the community. Today it just paralyzes people. Thus in future you actors can depict your characters so that one can imagine them behaving differently from the way they do, even when there are good grounds for their behaving in that particular way. You can set about outlining your characters much as when a bolder and more experienced engineer comes along and corrects his predecessor's drawings by superimposing new lines on the old ones, crossing out figures and replacing them by others, and scribbling critical remarks and comments. You can represent the famous opening scene in *Lear*, where he divides his kingdom between his daughters according to the measure of their love for him, and gets the measure quite wrong, in such a way that the audience says: 'He's going about it the wrong way. If only he hadn't said that, or had noticed this, or at any rate thought twice.'

THE PHILOSOPHER: What kind of thinking are we talking about? Is it thinking as opposed to feeling, the mere struggle to keep sober? Such an appeal to sobriety – like 'don't let's take decisions while under the influence' or 'better think it over' – is by no means misplaced given the activities of our stage magicians, but it's only a first step. We've already established that we need to get rid of the conviction that art cannot be appreciated till one abandons sobriety and approaches intoxication – we know that the whole gamut from sobriety to intoxication and the whole tension between the two extremes is present in the appreciation of art. Any effort to present scenes and characters so that they can be bloodlessly noted and weighed up would be quite unnecessary and even harmful for our purposes. All the premonitions, expectations, sympathies we bring to our real-life dealings with people should be aroused here too. The audience shouldn't see characters that are simply people who do their own particular deed, i.e. prepare their own entries, but human beings: shifting raw material, unformed and undefined, that can surprise them. It's only when confronted by such characters that they will practise true thinking; that is to say thinking that is conditioned by self-interest, and introduced and accompanied by feelings, a kind of thinking that displays every stage of awareness, clarity and effectiveness.

THE ACTOR: Aren't I bound hand and foot by the author's text?

THE PHILOSOPHER: You could treat the text as a report which is authentic but has several meanings. A vaguely defined Caesar, so you hear, surrounded by aristocratic assassins, is supposed to have murmured to a certain Brutus 'Et tu, Brute'. Anybody who hears a report like that, not by getting it in his lines but by some other means, hasn't learnt all that much; his knowledge of the world hasn't made very marked progress. Even if he is inclined to generalize he can do so in a number of false directions. Then you, the actor, burst into this vaguely nebulous conception and represent life itself. By the time you are through the audience ought to have seen even more than an eyewitness of the original incident.

THE DRAMATURG: What about plays of the imagination? Don't they only provide reports about the writer?

THE PHILOSOPHER: No, not only. You should treat them as reports of dreams or projects where the writer is again manipulating reality. Even if you have to look for what he must have seen then – find out what the point of his story can have been, and so on – there's still a good deal of elbow-room left you.

THE ACTOR: Surely you're not telling me I'm to imitate a character without having got inside it first ?

THE PHILOSOPHER: Several operations are needed to build up a character. In most cases you aren't imitating people you have seen, but must first imagine the persons you want to imitate. You start with what you can get from the text you are to speak, the actions and reactions that are prescribed for you and the situations through which your character is supposed to develop. Probably you'll have repeatedly to get inside the person you are representing, his situation, his physical characteristics, his modes of thought. It's one of the operations involved in building the character up. It's entirely consistent with our purposes, so long as you know how to get out of him again. There's a vast difference between somebody's having a picture of something, which demands imagination, and an illusion, which demands gullibility. We need imagination for our purposes; we want not to create illusions but to see that the audience too gets a picture of the matter in hand.

THE ACTOR: I fancy you've got an exaggerated view, which amounts almost to an illusion, of the degree to which we old-fashioned actors identify ourselves with our parts. I may as well tell you that when we play King Lear we think of all kinds of things that would hardly have entered Lear's mind.

THE PHILOSOPHER: I've no doubt. How can you bring out this and avoid that, and so on. Whether the props are in the right place and whether the comedian won't suddenly start waggling his ears again in the middle of your big speech. But all these thoughts are devoted to making sure that the audience doesn't wake up from its illusion. They may interfere with your empathy, but they only add to that of the audience. And to me it matters far more that the latter should be prevented than that the former should not be interfered with.

THE ACTOR: You mean that one ought only to get into the character's skin at rehearsals and not in the performance?

THE PHILOSOPHER: It's a bit difficult for me to answer. I could confine myself to saying that you oughtn't to get into his skin in the performance. I've every right to do so. First of all because I made a distinction between empathy and getting into the character, then because I really do believe empathy to be quite unnecessary, but above all because I'd be afraid that any other answer, whatever it was, might open a loophole for all the old trouble again just when I've barred the door to it. All the same I hesitate to. I can picture empathy occurring in marginal situations without any really harmful results. There is a series of steps by which they could be averted. The empathy would have to be interrupted and only take place at specific junctures, or else be very very weak and mixed in with other more forceful operations. I have actually seen acting of that sort – it was the last of a great number of rehearsals; everyone was tired, they only cared about memorizing text and positions, moved mechanically, spoke in a subdued voice and so on – where the effect satisfied me, though I could not be wholly certain whether the actors were experiencing empathy. But I must say the actors would never dare to play like that before an audience, that's to say so unemphatically and caring so little about effectiveness (on account of being so concentrated on 'externals'), and so probably the empathy, if there was any, only failed to jar because the playing lacked life. In short, if I could be sure you'd see no less vast a difference between the new kind of acting and the old kind based on complete empathy, were I to accept the possibility of a very slight modicum of empathy, then I'd accept it. Even then I'd judge your mastery according to how little empathy you managed with and not in the usual way according to how much you could generate.

THE DRAMATURG: Could we put it like this? At present people are called amateurs if they can't generate empathy; won't they one day be called amateurs if they can't do without it? But don't worry. You haven't made your method of acting seem any less strange to us by your judicious admission.

THE ACTOR: Does getting rid of empathy mean getting rid of every emotional element?

THE PHILOSOPHER: No, no. Neither the public nor the actor must be stopped from taking part emotionally; the representation of emotions must not be hampered, nor must the actor's use of emotions be frustrated. Only one out of many possible sources of emotion needs to be left unused, or at least treated as a subsidiary source – empathy.

Shakespeare's Theatre

THE DRAMATURG: A few years before the appearance of Shakespeare's first play Marlowe introduced iambic blank verse and so improved the popular plays of the time that even the connoisseurs came to accept them instead of the wooden pseudo-Seneca of more conventional writers. The counterpointing of two different plots, so brilliantly executed in *The Merchant of Venice*, was a technical innovation of that period. It was full of rapid, headlong and unhesitating progress of that sort. Plays were beginning to be treated as merchandise, but the conditions which governed property were still chaotic. Neither thoughts nor images, incidents, inspirations, discoveries were protected by law; the theatre was a source of discovery that was just like life. Its great personalities are its crude personalities polished up; its high-bred speech is vulgar speech refined. How much was concessions to the educated public in the boxes; how much concessions to the pit? Colleges depended on beer gardens and beer gardens on colleges.

THE DRAMATURG: There's a manuscript of a play of 1601 containing various alternative readings and a note by the author in the margin saying 'Choose whichever reading seems best to you' and 'If this way of putting it is difficult to understand or unsuited to the audience, then use another'.

THE DRAMATURG: Women are already going to the theatre, but the women's parts are still being played by boys. There are no backcloths, so the writer takes on the job of depicting the land-scape. The stage represents no specific area; it can be the whole extent of a heath.

Richard III Act V scene 3 shows two camps with the tents of Richard and Richmond and in between these a ghost appearing in a dream to the two men, visible and audible to each of them and addressing itself to both. A theatre full of A-effects!*

THE DRAMATURG: They were also theatres where people smoked. Tobacco was on sale in the auditorium. So you have snobs with pipes sitting on the stage and dreamily observing how the actor portrays Macbeth's death.

THE ACTOR: But isn't it essential to raise the theatre above the level of the street, and give its playing a particular stamp, since it doesn't in fact take place in the street or by accident and isn't performed by amateurs or occasioned by some incident ?

THE PHILOSOPHER: The factors you mention raise it as much as it needs, I'd say. All these differences between theatre and street scene ought to be particularly emphasized. Certainly nothing ought to be camouflaged away. But however clearly you differentiate the two kinds of demonstration, something of the everyday one's function is bound to be carried over into the theatrical. And it's precisely by underlining the element of difference, of professionalism, preparation and so on that you keep this function fresh.

THE DRAMATURG: Nothing gives us a better idea of the sober, healthy, profane state of the Elizabethan theatre than a look at Shakespeare's contracts with his companies, which guaranteed him a seventh part of the shares and a fourteenth part of the income of two theatres; at the cuts he made in his own plays, amounting to between a quarter and a third of all the verses; at his instructions to his actors (in *Hamlet*) to act in a restrained and natural manner. Add to that the fact that they acted (and also rehearsed, of course) by daylight in the open air, mostly without any attempt to indicate the place of the action and in

---

* (Trans.) For an explanation of A- or alienation-effects see p. 76.

the closest proximity to the audience, who sat on all sides, including on the stage, with a crowd standing or strolling around, and you'll begin to get an idea how earthly, profane and lacking in magic it all was.

THE ACTOR: So that *A Midsummer Night's Dream* was played in daylight and it was daylight when the ghost in Hamlet appeared? What price illusion?

THE DRAMATURG: People were supposed to use their imaginations.

THE DRAMATURG: What about tragedy in Shakespeare?

THE PHILOSOPHER: He takes a tragic view of the decline of feudalism. *Lear*, tied up in his own patriarchal ideas; *Richard III*, the unlikeable man who makes himself terrifying; *Macbeth*, the ambitious man swindled by witches; *Antony*, the hedonist who hazards his mastery of the world; *Othello*, destroyed by jealousy: they are all living in a new world and are smashed by it.

THE ACTOR: That explanation might spoil the plays for a lot of people.

THE PHILOSOPHER: But how could there be anything more complex, fascinating and important than the decline of great ruling classes?

THE DRAMATURG: Shakespeare's plays are extraordinarily full of life. Apparently they were printed from the prompt copy, and took in all the changes made at rehearsal and the actors' improvisations. The way the blank verse is set down suggests that it must in many cases have been done by ear. *Hamlet* has always interested me specially for the following reasons. We know it was adapted from a previous play by a certain Thomas Kyd that had had a great success a few years earlier. Its theme is the cleansing of an Augean stable. The hero, Hamlet, cleans up his family. He seems to have done so quite without inhibitions, and the last act is evidently meant to be the climax. The star of Shakespeare's Globe Theatre, however, was a stout man and short of breath, and so for a while all the heroes had to be stout and short of breath; this went for Macbeth as well as Lear. As a result the plot was deepened for him; and probably by him, too. Cascades and rapids were built in. The play became so much more interesting; it looks as if they must have re-modelled and readapted it on the stage as far as Act IV, then found themselves faced with the problem of how to bring this hesitant Hamlet up to the final ranting bloodbath that was the hit scene of the original play. Act IV contains a number of scenes each of which represents one possible solution. The actor may have needed to use the whole lot; or perhaps he only needed one, and the rest were none the less included in the book. They seem like so many bright ideas.

THE ACTOR: I suppose the plays may have been made like films are now.

THE DRAMATURG: Possibly. It must have been a really gifted writer who pinned them down in the book version, though.

THE ACTOR: From what you've said I'd picture Shakespeare coming along with a fresh scene every day.

THE DRAMATURG: Exactly. I feel they were experimenting. They were experimenting just as Galileo was experimenting in Florence at that time and Bacon in London. And so it is right to stage the plays in a spirit of experiment.

THE ACTOR. People think that's sacrilege.

THE DRAMATURG: If it weren't for sacrilege the plays wouldn't exist.

THE ACTOR: But as soon as you alter them in any way you're accused of treating them as less than perfect.

THE DRAMATURG: That's simply a mistaken idea of perfection.

THE PHILOSOPHER: The Globe Theatre's experiments and Galileo's experiments in treating the globe itself in a new way both reflected certain global transformations. The bourgeoisie was taking its first hesitant footsteps. Shakespeare could never have tailored the part to fit that short-winded character actor of his if the feudal family hadn't just collapsed. Hamlet's new bourgeois way of thinking is part of Hamlet's sickness. His experiments lead straight to disaster.

THE DRAMATURG: Not straight. Zigzag.

THE PHILOSOPHER: All right; zigzag. In a sense the play has the permanence of something makeshift, and I agree that that probably has to be resolved if we're to preserve it.

THE ACTOR: So what we're to try and show is things like *So-far-and-no-further* or *no-further-but-so-far*. That's slightly different from the old-fashioned system of unlimited ranting ending up in total collapse. There's an element of *relativity* there which you want us to take into account which is bound to have less powerful effects than absolute black-and-white. If I show a man as relatively ambitious nobody's likely to go along with it in the same way as if I showed him wholly and utterly ambitious.

THE PHILOSOPHER: But in real life people are more often relatively ambitious than wholly and utterly ambitious, aren't they?

THE ACTOR: Maybe. But it's a question of what's effective.

THE PHILOSOPHER: You must achieve that with something that's less unlikely to happen in real life. That's your business.

THE ACTOR: A nice Macbeth that would make: sometimes ambitious and sometimes not, and only relatively more ambitious than Duncan And your Hamlet: very hesitant, but also very inclined to act too hastily, no? And Clytemnestra: relatively vindictive. Romeo: relatively in love. . . .

THE DRAMATURG: Yes, more or less. You needn't laugh. In Shakespeare he's already in love before he's seen his Juliet at all. After that he's more in love.

THE ACTOR: Ha, a bursting scrotum! As if other people didn't suffer from that besides Romeo, and without being Romeos.

THE PHILOSOPHER: All the same, Romeo has got one. It's one of Shakespeare's great realistic strokes to notice that.

THE ACTOR: And Richard III's unholy fascination: how can I show that except by making it fill the whole of the character?

THE DRAMATURG: You mean, in the scene where he so fascinates the widow of the man he's murdered that she becomes his victim? I can see two solutions. Either she must be shown to be terrified into it, or else she must be made to be ugly. But however you show his fascination it won't do you any good unless you can show how she fails him later in the play. So you have to show a relative power of fascination.

THE PHILOSOPHER: Oh, you show that already. But it's like a trumpeter showing brass or an apple tree in winter showing snow. You're confusing two things: showing something, and having people come across it.

THE DRAMATURG: Have we got to scrap all those marvellous old plays, then?

THE PHILOSOPHER: I wouldn't say so.

THE ACTOR: What about *King Lear*?

THE PHILOSOPHER: It's partly a report on the way people lived together in a previous age. All you've got to do is put the report into effect.

THE DRAMATURG: A lot of people think such plays ought to be performed as they stand, and claim that it would be barbarism to make any change in them.

THE PHILOSOPHER: But it's a barbaric play. Of course, you need to go about it very carefully if you're not to spoil its beauty. If you're going to perform it on the new principle so that the audience doesn't feel completely identified with this king, then you can stage very nearly the whole play, with minor additions to encourage the audience to keep their heads. What you cannot have is the audience, including those who happen to be servants themselves, taking Lear's side to such an extent that they applaud when a servant gets beaten for carrying out his mistress's orders as happens in Act I scene 4.

THE ACTOR: How are you to stop it?

THE DRAMATURG: Say he was beaten and injured, then staggered out with every sign of having been hurt. That would change their attitude.

THE ACTOR: Then you'd have people turning against Lear for reasons associated with purely modern times.

THE DRAMATURG: Not if you're consequential about it. The servants of this generally unwanted king could be shown as a little group which no longer gets its meals anywhere and pursues him with dumb reproaches. Lear would have to wince at the sight of them, and that would be a good enough reason for him to lose his temper. You just have to show the feudal conditions.

THE ACTOR: In that case you might as well take his division of his kingdom seriously and have an actual map torn up in the first scene. Lear could hand the pieces to his daughters in the hope of ensuring their love that way. He could take the third piece, the one meant for Cordelia, and tear that across once again to distribute to the others. That would be a particularly good way of making the audience stop and think.

THE DRAMATURG: But you'd destroy the play, because you'd be starting something that led nowhere.

THE PHILOSOPHER: Perhaps it does lead somewhere; we'd have to look at the play. In any case, it wouldn't hurt if there were some abnormal episodes of this sort, hotbeds of inconsistency that one suddenly stumbled into. The old reports are full of such things. It's already impossible to perform these medieval plays to audiences that don't have any historical sense. That's sheer folly. But Shakespeare is a great realist, and I think he'd stand the test. He always shovels a lot of raw material on to the stage, unvarnished representations of what he has seen. And there are those useful junction points in his works where the new in his period collided with the old. We too are at one and the same time fathers of a new period and sons of an old one; we understand a great deal of the remote past and can still share once overwhelming feelings which were stimulated on a grand scale. And the society in which we live is a very complex one, too. Man is the sum of all the social conditions of all times, as the classics* have it. All the same, there is a lot in these works that is dead, distorted and empty. This can continue to be printed; for all we know it may be shamming dead, and it may anyway explain other aspects of this past period. I would almost sooner draw your attention to the wealth of living elements still to be found in such works at apparently dead junctures. An infinitesimal addition, and they spring to life, specifically now, specifically not till now. What really matters is to play these old works historically, which means setting them in

* (Trans.) i.e. the Marxist classics.

powerful contrast to our own time. For it is only against the background of our time that their shape emerges as an old shape, and without this background I doubt if they could have any shape at all.

THE DRAMATURG: How about the old masterpieces?

THE PHILOSOPHER: The classic attitude I saw was that of an old worker from a textile factory, who saw a very ancient knife lying on my desk, a rustic table-knife I used to cut pages with. He picked up this lovely object in his great wrinkled hands, half shut his eyes to look at its small silver-chased hardwood handle and narrow blade, and said: 'Fancy them making a thing like that in the days when they still believed in witches.' I clearly saw that he was proud of such fine work. 'They make better steel now,' he went on, 'but look how beautifully it balances. Nowadays they make knives just like hammers; nobody'd think of weighing the handle against the blade. Of course, someone probably spent several days tinkering about with that. It'd take half a second nowadays, but the job's not so good.'

THE ACTOR: He saw everything that was beautiful about it?

THE PHILOSOPHER: Everything. He had that kind of sixth sense for history.

Piscator's Theatre

THE DRAMATURG: In the period after the First World War, before the housepainter came on the scene, Piscator opened his theatre in Berlin. A lot of people think he was one of the theatre's greatest men. He got the money from a brewer, who thought that a theatre, seeing how hard it was to check its income and its expenditure, might help him fox the tax-collector. His experiments cost more than a million marks. For each new play he put on he would rebuild the theatre, not just the stage. The stage, however, was where he effected the greatest changes. He made the floor move by covering it with two broad bands that could be set in motion by a motor, so that the actors could march up and down without budging from where they were. He made a whole play flow by these means. The play showed a soldier marching to the front, through recruiting office, hospital and barracks, along country roads, through camps and cowsheds into battle. It showed how the soldier was marched off by his superiors, but how he kept on crossing their plans, apparently carrying out all their orders but never actually getting to the battlefield. As a background to the same play he used a cartoon film caricaturing those superiors. Indeed it was he who first introduced films into the theatre, and thereby turned the set into an actor. There was another play where he had two overlapping revolving stages on which he built up several scenes of action with the actors performing there simultaneously. Stage and roof both began to sag; it was the first time that that theatre or any other had had to support machines.

THE DRAMATURG: Piscator's theatre, run with money from a brewer and a cinema proprietor, of whom one had an actress girl-friend and the other was just socially ambitious, was frequented almost exclusively by grand bourgeois, proletarians and intellectuals. The stalls were extremely expensive, the gallery extremely cheap; part of the proletarian audience took season tickets. This part represented a severe financial handicap, since the large amount of machinery made the settings very expensive. It was an up-to-date theatre, not only when dealing with topical questions but also when its problems were hundreds of years old. A team of playwrights used to conduct a more or less non-stop discussion on the stage, and this discussion continued right through the whole immense city in newspapers, drawing-rooms, pubs and cafés. There was no theatrical censorship; social contrasts were sharply marked and becoming more so. The big bourgeoisie was frightened of the Junker class, who still held the leading positions in the army and the civil service; the workers were fighting petty-bourgeois tendencies within their own parties. Piscator's theatre provided them with object-lessons. Here one could see how the 1918 revolution had fizzled out; how wars had been provoked by the struggle for markets and raw materials; how these wars had been fought by using the peoples against their will; how successful revolutions had been made. The theatre *qua* artistic institution altered drastically with each new task it undertook; at times it had remarkably little to do with art. The insertion of all kinds of demonstrations broke up the story and the development of the characters; there were harsh alternations of declamation and everyday language, play and film, acting and public speaking. The background, which had previously been a motionless extra, (and in the other neighbouring theatres still was), became the theatre's main star and hogged the limelight. It consisted of a cinema screen. Shots of topical events, extracted from the newsreels, were strung significantly together to provide the documentary material. The boards themselves were made to move. Two endless belts driven by motors made it possible to play scenes on the street. There were speaking and singing choruses on the stage. The plans made were just as important as the finished or half-finished article (for one never saw anything really finished). I'll give you a couple of instances. For the production of a play about the cruelty of the abortion law a particular house in a slum district was to have been reproduced on the stage so exactly as to include every single blackleaded stovepipe. In the intervals the audience was to have been allowed to make a detailed inspection of it. Then there was to have been a play about the Chinese revolution with a number of banners on sticks bearing short painted slogans about the situation. ('Textile workers out on strike.' 'Revolutionary meetings among the small peasants.' 'Shopkeepers buying weapons' and so on.) They were supposed to have inscriptions on the back as well, so that they could be turned round to show other slogans as a background to the incidents on the stage. ('Strike collapses.' 'Small peasants forming armed squads' and so forth.) By such means continually altering situations could be made recognizable; it could be shown how one element persists after another has already altered, and so on.*

When it came to the performance this system of mobile signals was not put into effect. The paper flags were indeed inscribed back and front,

THE DRAMATURG: Piscator was one of the greatest theatre men of all time. He electrified the theatre and made it capable of mastering great subjects. He was not so wholly uninterested in acting as his enemies said; none the less he was more so than he himself gave out. Possibly he failed to share their interests because they failed to share his. At any rate, he established no new style for them, even though he was not bad at showing how a part should be acted, particularly small and sharply etched ones. He tolerated several different ways of acting on his stage at the same time: not really a sign of specially good taste. He found it easier to master great subjects critically by means of ingenious and spectacular scenic presentation than by the actors' art. His love of machinery, which let him in for frequent blame and occasional excesses of praise, was something he only showed when it allowed him to use his scenic imagination. He had a marked appreciation of simplicity – which incidentally led him to describe the Augsburger's* style of writing as coming closest to his own intentions – which corresponded to the simplicity of his objective: to expose the world's mechanism on a grand scale and to copy it in such a way that it would be more easily serviced.

---

but only so that they could be changed around between scenes and made use of twice. During the first performance Piscator and the present writer walked round outside, as usual at first performances, and discussed what had been achieved at rehearsal and what had gone wrong, largely ignoring what was going on in the theatre, since a great deal had been altered at the last moment and was now having to be extemporized. In the course of this conversation they discovered the principle of the system of mobile signals, its possibilities for the drama and its significance for the style of representation. Often there were experimental results like this which the audience never saw on account of the lack of time and money, but which none the less simplified subsequent operations and at any rate influenced the views of the experimenters themselves.

* (Trans.) Brecht was born and brought up in Augsburg. In the German edition this half-humorous term for himself which he employed in the original manuscripts has been changed to 'the playwright' in accordance with a pencilled note of his. In English the meaning is clearer if this is not done.

The Third Night

FRAGMENTS FROM THE THIRD NIGHT

The Augsburger's Theatre

THE DRAMATURG: Piscator was making political theatre before the Augsburger. He had taken part in the war, the Augsburger not. The 1918 revolution, in which both took part, had made the Augsburger disillusioned and turned Piscator into a politician. It was only later that the Augsburger came to politics through study. At the time when their collaboration began each of them had his theatre, Piscator one of his own Am Nollendorfplatz and the Augsburger one Am Schiffbauerdamm, where he trained his actors. The Augsburger revised most of Piscator's major plays for him, wrote scenes for them and on one occasion an entire act. *Schweik* he did for him entirely. Conversely Piscator supported the Augsburger and used to come to his rehearsals. Both preferred working with a team. They had collaborators in common: Eisler the composer, for instance, and Grosz the draughtsman. Both got great artists to work with amateurs and performed revues to the workers. Though Piscator never wrote a play himself and hardly ever even wrote a scene, the Augsburger claimed that apart from himself he was the only competent dramatist. He would ask if Piscator hadn't proved that plays can also be made by inspiring scenes and projects by other writers, supplying them with documents and scenic performances, and making a montage of them. The actual theory of the non-Aristotelian theatre and the development of the A-effect should be credited to the Augsburger, but much of it was also applied by Piscator, and in a wholly original and independent way. Above all, the theatre's conversion to politics was Piscator's achievement, without which the Augsburger's theatre would hardly be conceivable.*

THE DRAMATURG: Before the Augsburger took up the theatre he studied the natural sciences and medicine. For him the arts and the sciences were opposites on the same plane. Both occupations had to make themselves useful. He didn't despise the usefulness of the arts, like many of his contemporaries, and he allowed the sciences not to bother about usefulness if they wished. He considered that they too were arts.

THE DRAMATURG: He was a young man when the First World War ended. He studied medicine in southern Germany. Two writers and a popular comedian were the chief influences on him. In those years the writer *Büchner*, who had written in the 1830s, was performed for the first time, and the Augsburger saw the unfinished play *Woyzeck*: he also saw the writer *Wedekind* performing his own works in a style which he had developed in cabaret. Wedekind had worked as a ballad singer; he accompanied himself on the lute. But the man he learnt most from was the clown *Valentin*, who performed in a beer-hall. He did short sketches in which he played refractory employees, orchestral musicians or photographers, who hated their employer and made him look ridiculous. The employer was played by his partner, a popular woman comedian who used to pad herself out and speak in a deep bass voice. When the Augsburger was producing his first play, which included a thirty minutes' battle, he asked Valentin what he ought to do

---

* (Trans.) There are points on which the reader might be misled by this speech. (*a*) At the time in question (*c.* 1928–9) the Theater am Schiffbauerdamm was actually directed by Ernst-Josef Aufricht. (*b*) Hašek's *Schweik* was produced by Piscator in an adaptation by Max Brod and Hans Reimann and though Brecht worked on it he was never credited with the play; it is the only time he appears to make this claim. (*c*) George Grosz never designed a Brecht play or production, though he illustrated his poem *Die Drei Soldaten* (1931).

with the soldiers. 'What are soldiers like in battle?' Valentin promptly answered: 'White. Scared.'

THE DRAMATURG: The Augsburger's theatre was very small. It performed very few plays. It trained very few actors. The chief actresses were Weigel, Neher and Lenya. The chief actors were Homolka, Lorre and Lingen. The singer Busch likewise belonged to this theatre, but he seldom appeared on the stage. The chief scene designer was Caspar Neher, no relation to the actress. The musicians were Weill and Eisler.

Audiences in the Weimar republic weren't strong enough to provide actors with real fame. So the Augsburger set out to give all his actors as much fame as possible in their own eyes. There is a little didactic poem, for instance, in which he tells Neher how she ought to wash herself each morning, like a famous person in such a way that artists could paint it. They were all reasonably famous, but came before the audience on the stage as if they were a great deal more so, that is to say modestly.

THE DRAMATURG: The Augsburger drew a very clear line between mistakes that came from ignoring his rules and those which came despite or even because of their observation. 'My rules,' he used to say, 'can only be applied by people who have acquired a contradictory spirit, independence of judgement, and social imagination, and are in contact with the progressive elements in the audience, which means being themselves progressive, wide-awake, thinking persons. That being so, it's not for me to muzzle the threshing ox. My actors accordingly make a whole series of mistakes which don't represent any infringement of my rules, since these don't apply to every area of their behaviour. There were evenings when even Weigel burst into tears at certain points, quite against her own will and by no means to the advantage of the performance. In one play she took the part of a peasant woman in the Spanish civil war and had to curse her son and wish him dead because she thought he had taken up arms against the generals; (in point of fact he had already been shot by the generals' troops, and while peacefully fishing at that). The civil war was still being fought when this performance took place. It is not clear whether the war had taken an unfavourable turn for the oppressed that day or Weigel had some other reason for being in a specially sensitive mood, but anyway that day as she spoke her curse against the murdered man the tears began to flow. She wasn't weeping as a peasant, but as a performer and for the peasant. I see that as a mistake, but I don't see any offence against my rules.'

THE ACTOR: But her weeping wasn't acted! It was purely her own affair!

THE DRAMATURG: True. But the Augsburger rejected the audience's demand that the actor should be wholly absorbed in his part. His actors weren't waiters who must serve up the meat and have their private, personal feelings treated as gross importunities. They were servants neither of the writer nor of the audience. His actors weren't officials of a political movement, and they weren't high priests of art. Their job as political human beings was to use art or anything else to further their social cause. Spoiling the illusion, moreover, was something the Augsburger judged leniently. He was against illusion. On his stage there were private jokes, improvisations and extemporizations such as would have been unthinkable in the old theatre.

THE PHILOSOPHER: Mightn't he also have felt that treating such accidental, unacted, arbitrary conduct on the part of his actors so leniently was a way of discrediting their authority? They weren't supposed to stamp their conceptions as incontrovertible, if I've got the picture right.

THE DRAMATURG: Certainly not.

THE DRAMATURG: I've turned your ideas over in my mind and they've picked up one or two points there. A few years back when I was visiting Paris I went to a small theatre where a tiny group of German exiles were acting a few scenes from a play showing conditions at home. I've never come across a group whose members were so widely varied in background, training and talents. There was a working man who could hardly have set foot on a stage before and spoke in dialect, and alongside him a great actress whose resources, gifts and stage education are possibly unrivalled. They had two things in common: the fact that they had all fled their country in face of the housepainter's hordes' and a particular style of acting. It's a style that must be very close to the sort of approach to theatre you yourself have conceived.

THE PHILOSOPHER: Describe their acting.

THE DRAMATURG: The play they were performing was called *Fear and Misery of the Third Reich*. I was told it consisted of twenty-four little plays, of which they performed seven or eight. These plays showed how the people in your country are behaving under the housepainter's rod of iron. You saw people of pretty well all classes, and how they resisted or knuckled under. You saw the fear of the oppressed and the fear of the oppressors. It was like a great collection of gestures, observed with artistry: the quarry looking back over his shoulder (and the pursuer's look too); the sudden silences; the hand that flies to one's own mouth when one is about to say too much, and the hand that falls on the wanted man's shoulder; the extorted lie, the whispered truth, the mutual distrust of lovers, and much more. But what was so unusual was that the players never performed these ghastly episodes in such a way that the spectators were tempted to call out 'Stop'. The spectators didn't seem in any way to share the horror of those on the stage, and as a result there was repeatedly laughter among the audience without doing any damage to the profoundly serious character of the performance. For this laughter seemed to apply to the stupidity that found itself having to make use of force, and to the helplessness that took the shape of brutality. Bullies were seen as men tripping over, criminals as men who have made a mistake or allowed themselves to be taken in. The spectators' laughter was finely graduated. It was a happy laughter when the quarry outwitted his pursuer, a contented laughter when somebody uttered a good, true word. That's how an inventor might laugh on finding the solution after a long effort: it was as obvious as that, and he took so long to see it!

THE ACTOR: How did they manage that?

THE DRAMATURG: It isn't entirely easy to say, but I didn't get the impression that it was all that difficult. The main thing was that they acted in such a way that the audience's interest was always focused on the ensuing development, the further continuation: as it were, on the mechanics of the episodes. On the interplay of cause and effect.

THE DRAMATURG: It seems to me that your liking for folk pictures has rather diverted us from that desire of the audience for knowledge on which you want to base your way of making theatre. These pictures are out to make one's flesh creep. About earthquakes, fires, atrocities and the blows of fate.

THE PHILOSOPHER: We've not been diverted, only gone back; the essence of this folk art is insecurity. The earth quakes and opens up. The roof suddenly goes up in flames. Kings are menaced by a change of fortune. And insecurity is at the root of desire for knowledge too. The signals for rescue and redress may be richer or poorer according to mankind's ability to help itself.

THE DRAMATURG: So it's possible to enjoy insecurity?

THE PHILOSOPHER: Remember the English saying: 'It's an ill wind that blows nobody any good.' People want to be made just as insecure as they really are.

THE DRAMATURG: You don't want to get rid of this element of insecurity in art, then?

THE PHILOSOPHER: Not by any manner of means.

THE ACTOR: So it's back to pity and terror after all?

THE PHILOSOPHER: Don't jump to conclusions. I'm reminded of a photograph which one of the American steel companies used for a newspaper advertisement. It showed Yokohama after its destruction by an earthquake. A jumble of houses that had collapsed on top of each other. Between them, however, still towered one or two fairly tall buildings of reinforced concrete. Underneath was written 'Steel stood'.

THE ACTOR: Lovely.

THE DRAMATURG to the Worker: What are you laughing for?

THE WORKER: Because it's lovely.

THE PHILOSOPHER: That photograph was an unmistakable tip to art.

THE ACTOR: This notion of continually observing oneself and referring back to one's own experience can easily lead a man to alter the text. What's your view of that?

THE PHILOSOPHER: What does the Augsburger say?

THE DRAMATURG: Actors are usually very self-centred about amendments. They see nothing but their own parts. The result is that they not only answer questions but alter questions in such a way that the answers are no longer valid. If such alterations are made collectively, and with no less a degree of interest and talent than has gone into the actual writing of the play, then it will be to the play's advantage. One shouldn't overlook the fact that it's not the play but the performance that is the real purpose of all one's efforts. Alterations demand a great deal of art, that's all.

THE PHILOSOPHER: That last sentence seems to me to define the limits well enough. I'd like also to point out that too great an inclination to make changes may make for a frivolous study of the text, but on the other hand that the possibility of alteration, and the knowledge that this may be essential, make its study deeper.

THE DRAMATURG: The important thing is that if one is going to alter one must have the courage and the competence to alter enough. I remember a performance of Schiller's *Die Räuber* at Piscator's theatre. The company felt that as one of the robbers, Spiegelberg, was an extremist Schiller had been wrong in making him seem disagreeable to the audience. As a result he was played agreeably, and the play literally fell apart. For neither action nor dialogue gave any pretext for suggesting that Spiegelberg's behaviour is agreeable. The play made a reactionary impact (which it shouldn't if you look at it historically), while Spiegelberg's tirades failed to make a revolutionary one. It would have taken the most extensive alterations, carried out with considerable art and a feeling for history, for there to have been the slightest chance of presenting Spiegelberg's outlook, which is more extreme than that of the principal character, as the more progressive.

THE DRAMATURG: As we've seen, the Augsburger cuts his plays up into a series of little independent playlets, so that the action progresses by jumps. He doesn't like scenes to slide imperceptibly into one another. So how does he cut, then, and from what points of view? He does it in such a way that each individual scene can be given a title of a historical or social-political or anthropological kind.

THE ACTRESS: For instance?

THE DRAMATURG: 'Mother Courage goes to war as a tradeswoman', or 'Mother Courage is in a hurry because she's afraid the war may end suddenly', or 'As she is entertaining the recruiting sergeant one of his men takes her son off.'

THE ACTOR: What's historical or social-political or anthropological about the last of these titles?

THE DRAMATURG: The play shows it to be typical of the period that kind actions can prove expensive.

THE ACTOR: It's typical of our own period too, and was there ever a period when it was different?

THE DRAMATURG: We might be able to represent one.

THE DRAMATURG: The Augsburger filmed Weigel making herself up. He cut the film up, and each frame showed a complete facial expression, self-contained and with its own meaning. 'You see what sort of actress she is,' he said admiringly. 'Each gesture can be analysed into as many gestures as you like, and all of them perfect. Everything is there for the sake of something else, and at the same time for its own. Not only the jump is beautiful but also the run-up.' But what mattered most to him was that every movement of the muscles as she made up brought about a perfect expression of her personality. The people he showed these pictures to, asking them what the various expressions meant, suggested such things as anger, gaiety, envy, compassion. He showed them to Weigel too, telling her that she only needed to know her own expressions in order to be able to express the various moods without always having to feel them.

The A-effect

THE PHILOSOPHER: If empathy makes something ordinary of a special event, alienation makes something special of an ordinary one. The most hackneyed everyday incidents are stripped of their monotony when represented as quite special. The audience is no longer taking refuge from the present day in history; the present day becomes history.

THE PHILOSOPHER: The main reason why the actor has to be clearly detached from his character is this: if the audience is to be shown how to handle the character, or if people who resemble it or are in similar situations are to be shown the secret of their problems, then he must adopt a standpoint which is not only outside the character's radius but also at a more advanced stage of evolution. The classics* say that apes are best understood from the point of view of their successor in the evolutionary process, man.

THE DRAMATURG: There's no A-effect when the actor adopts another's facial expression at the cost of erasing his own. What he should do is to show the two faces overlapping.

The Actress plays a man

THE PHILOSOPHER: If a man had been playing that man he'd hardly have brought out his masculinity so forcibly; but because a woman played him (played the episode, to be more precise) we realized that a lot of details which we usually think of as general human characteristics are typically masculine. When it's a matter of sex, therefore, actors must show something of what an actress would bring to the interpretation of a

* (Trans.) Marxist again.

76

man, and actresses something of what an actor would bring to that of a woman.

THE ACTOR: I must say I've seldom seen such feminine women as at the front during the war, as played by men.

THE ACTRESS: And you ought to see grown-ups played by children. So much of grown-up behaviour strikes one as odd and alien then. I once saw schoolchildren doing the play *Mann ist Mann*. An elephant gets sold in it. This is an incident which would be impossible among children, and it suddenly became tinged with something of this impossibility in the play; at least, it came to seem barely possible, just conceivable, to be imagined under certain quite temporary conditions perhaps.

THE DRAMATURG: There was a further instance of the A-effect in an American film I saw. A very young actor who till then had always played working-class youths (and probably been one himself) played the part of a bourgeois youth who is given a dinner jacket for his first dance. He was a middle-class youth all right, but an extra-specially middle-class youth. Most of the audience probably only saw that he was an extra-specially youthful one. And it's a fact that the difference between young and old in the two classes is not the same. In some ways the working-class youth is more grown up than the bourgeois one, in others more childish.

THE DRAMATURG: Doesn't the *surrealist* movement in painting also use a technique of alienation?

THE PHILOSOPHER: Certainly. These refined and complex painters are so to speak the primitives of a new art form. They try to shock the observer by hampering, confusing and disappointing his associations; for instance, by making a woman's hand have eyes instead of fingers. The shock indeed occurs, both when this is treated symbolically (a woman seeing with her hands) and when it's just a matter of her extremities not living up to expectations, and hand and eye are alienated. The fact that the hand has ceased to be a hand gives rise to a conception of 'hand' which has more to do with this instrument's everyday functions than the piece of aesthetic decoration which we've seen on ten thousand canvases. Admittedly such pictures are often a reaction against the incomplete lack of function that people and things are liable to have in our period; in other words they are evidence of severe functional disturbance. A further sign of the same thing is the complaint that everything has got to function: i.e. that it's all a means and not an end.

THE DRAMATURG: How does this come to be a primitive application to the A-effect?

THE PHILOSOPHER: Because such art's function is likewise socially hamstrung, so that art simply stops functioning too. So far as results are concerned it finishes up as shock for entertainment's sake.

THE PHILOSOPHER: Take the death of the villain. The destruction of the anti-social figure to save lives. By some means or other the necessity of this destruction has to be disputed. It may be society's ultimate resort, but may not other resorts have been overlooked? The right to life, which society enforces so crudely that it cannot enforce it without denying it, is the basic right on which all other rights depend. We have to stand by the dying man in his struggle for this life; for the mere right to breathe, independent of all social enlargements and enrichments; simply for the metabolic process, for a vegetable existence. He doesn't want to die; he doesn't want to cease to be human; reduced to this extreme minimum his humanity is something that we have to respect because it's what we share with him, even if at the very same moment we are sharing in his inhumanity, by killing him or wishing to kill him. Oh, there's a lot that we share, even now. Something of the helplessness of our attitude to him was in him too. If lives are worth anything, it is for and by means of society.

THE PHILOSOPHER: Suppose you've a play where the first scene shows A bringing B to justice, then the process is reversed in the last scene and, after all kinds of incidents have been shown, B brings A to justice, so that there's one and the same process (bringing to justice) with A and B exchanging their respective roles (executioner and victim). In such a case you'll undoubtedly arrange the first scene so as to give the maximum possible effectiveness to the last. You'll ensure that on seeing the last scene the audience will immediately be reminded of the first; that the similarity will be striking; and at the same time that the differences will not be overlooked.

THE DRAMATURG: Such things are certainly done. Above all, in such a case the first scene oughtn't to be played as a transition to the next; it must be given a weight of its own. Every movement in it must be planned in relation to the same (or altered) movement in the last scene.

THE PHILOSOPHER: And an actor who knows that later on he's going to have to change places with his colleague is likely to act differently from one who doesn't, I'd say. He will represent the executioner differently if he remembers that he's going to have to represent the victim too.

THE DRAMATURG: Obviously.

THE PHILOSOPHER: So the last scene alienates the first (in the same way as the first alienates the last, which is the real gimmick of the play). The actor makes preparations that lead to A-effects. So now all you have to do is to apply this way of representation to plays where this last scene is missing.

THE DRAMATURG: You mean play all the scenes with reference to other potential scenes?

THE PHILOSOPHER: Yes.

THE PHILOSOPHER: The more concretely a case is put before him, the easier it is for a spectator to abstract ('Lear behaves like that.' 'Do I behave the same way?') One special father can be fathers in general. The specialness is a mark of generality. It's general to find something special.

THE PHILOSOPHER: Our wish to show society specific incidents in such a way that society can resolve specific anomalies should not lead us to neglect whatever lies outside its area of influence. Nor is it the case that we've simply to propound riddles, soluble and insoluble. The unknown can only develop from the known.

THE PHILOSOPHER: You can judge the extent of a law by the extent of the qualifications hedging it round. You shouldn't seek examples of it in unduly suitable and obliging types, but preferably in those who (within reason) dig in their heels. The types selected must be in some measure approximate. If, for instance, you think that a peasant acts in a specific way in the given circumstances, then take a quite specific peasant and not one who has been selected or fabricated for his willingness to act in precisely that way. It's better still if you can show the law applying differently to different peasants. Laws only provide you with extremely broad averages, summaries, guides. The concept 'class' for example is a concept that embraces a great number of individuals and thereby deprives them of their individuality. There are certain laws that apply to class. They apply to the individual only in so far as he coincides with his class, i.e. not absolutely; for the concept of class is only arrived at by ignoring particular features of the individual. You're not representing principles, but human beings.

THE DRAMATURG: The difference between a scientific representation of a rhinoceros – a drawing in a natural history book, for instance – and an artistic one lies in the fact that the latter suggests something of the artist's relation to the animal. His drawing contains stories even if it represents the animal and nothing more. The beast looks idle or angry or mangy or cunning. He will have included a number of characteristics which we don't need to know for the mere study of its anatomy.

THE DRAMATURG: Take the scene where *Lear* dies: his 'Pray you, undo this button: thank you, Sir!' A wish insinuates itself among his maledictions; life has become intolerable, and on top of that his clothes are too tight; it was a king that lived, a man who dies. He is quite polite: ('thank you, Sir'). The subject is fully covered in detail and in outline. A disappointed man is dying: dying and disappointment are shown, but don't quite coincide. There's no question of forgiveness, but friendly actions are not rejected. The man has gone too far, not so the dramatist.

Lear's destruction is complete; there is a startling last demonstration of death as a special horror; Lear really and truly dies.

THE ACTOR: It's one of the greatest achievements of the arts, however, that their images are not formed in accordance with the dictates of utility, taking into account the moral standards of the time, and confirming the ruling views.

THE DRAMATURG: Just a minute! If such images fail to confirm the ruling views, in other words, fail to respect the views of the rulers, they can none the less obey the dictates of utility. It may even become easier.

THE ACTOR: The arts go farther, though; or not so far, if you like. They are in a position to make something enjoyable of the power, beauty and majesty of the headlong river which can flood entire villages. They get enjoyment from the observation of anti-social individuals, showing the murderer's vitality, the swindler's cunning, the harpy's beauty.

THE PHILOSOPHER: That's all in order; such disorder is in order. So long as you don't conceal the flooded villages, blame the murderer's victims, tolerate the swindle and present the harpy's claw as a cleverly designed utensil, it'll all be in order.

THE ACTOR: I can't represent both butcher *and* sheep.

THE DRAMATURG: You're not the only person in the company, you know.

THE PHILOSOPHER: You can't represent butcher and sheep simultaneously, but you can still represent the butcher of the sheep, I fancy.

THE ACTOR: Am I to appeal to the mutton-eater in every spectator or to the man with an overdraft?

THE PHILOSOPHER: Mutton-eaters can have overdrafts too.

THE ACTOR: True enough, but you can't appeal to both qualities at once. No, I'm addressing the individual simply as a member of the whole of humanity. Humanity as a whole is interested in vitality as such, irrespective of what its effects may be.

THE DRAMATURG: Every character is built up from its relationship to the other characters. That means that an actor has to be as interested in his partner's playing as in his own.

THE ACTOR: Nothing new in that. I never steal my partner's thunder.

THE ACTRESS: Not always.

THE DRAMATURG: That's not the point at issue.

THE DRAMATURG: Note the difference between *strong* and *crude*, *relaxed* and *loose*, *quick* and *hurried*, *imaginative* and *distracting*, *thought out* and *concocted*, *deep-felt* and *emotional*, *contradictory* and *nonsensical*, *clear* and *emphatic*, *useful* and *profitable*, *rhetorical* and *boastful*, *stately* and *pompous*, *delicate* and *feeble*, *passionate* and *uncontrolled*, *natural* and *accidental*.

THE PHILOSOPHER: When the married man comes home and sees the *four-legged animal* in his bed the variety of sensations which he feels and displays are both consistent and not. The triumph of discovery ('Got here in the nick of time'): reluctance to discover something he doesn't like ('Can I believe my eyes?'): disgust at the pleasures of the flesh ('Like animals!'): gloomy comprehension of human needs ('She's got to have it'): the feeling of contemptuous renunciation ('I can't lose much if that's how things are'): the thirst for revenge ('I'll make her pay for it!') and so forth and so on.

THE DRAMATURG: Why is it that middle-class people always reproached the Augsburger* with having too little feeling and wishing to eliminate everything emotional in favour of the rational?

THE PHILOSOPHER: His use of reason stirred no emotions in their souls. Indeed, their feelings rebelled against him and his reason. They found him far too critical. Yet he wasn't appealing to their reason, but to that of their enemies. Also, he saw criticism as only a part of more practical measures to alter things. He would collect complaints about the course of river beds and the taste of apples as one part of an undertaking whose other part was damming up the rivers and improving the apple trees. His criticism was something practical, and hence im-

* (Trans.) Brecht says 'der Messingkäufer' – the man who is buying brass (as on page 15).

mediately emotional too, whereas their idea of criticism was associated with ethics rather than practical matters, and was thus restricted to the emotional sphere. Thus their criticism was very largely unfruitful, and this led them to stamp as un-fruitful everything that was critical, including his critical side.

THE DRAMATURG: I thought the misunderstanding was just that his objections to empathy in art were taken as objections to feeling in art.

THE PHILOSOPHER: No, the misunderstanding went deeper than that. In his day the bourgeoisie was always claiming that the rebellious masses were too emotionally confused to see how reasonable the existing order of society was, and accusing the masses' leaders of relying only on cold reason instead of on that emotional life which the people had developed over thousands of years: its religious, moral and family feelings.

The Fourth Night

The Playwright's Speech about the Theatre of the Stage Designer Caspar Neher

We often begin rehearsing without any knowledge of the stage designs, and our friend merely prepares small sketches of the episodes to be played (for instance, six people grouped around a working-class woman, who is upbraiding them). Perhaps we then find that in the text there are only five people in all, for our friend is no pedant; but he shows us the essential, and a sketch of this sort is always a small and delicate work of art. Whereabouts on the stage the woman is to sit, and her son and her guests, is something we find out for ourselves, and that is where our friend seats them when he comes to construct the set. Sometimes we get his designs beforehand, and then he helps us with groupings and gestures; not infrequently also with the differentiation of the characters and the way they speak. His set is steeped in the atmosphere of the play, and arouses the actor's ambition to take his place in it.

He reads plays in a masterly fashion. Take just one example. In *Macbeth*, Act I, scene 6, Duncan and his general Banquo, invited by Macbeth to his castle, praise the castle in the famous lines:

> *This guest of summer,*
> *The temple-haunting martlet does approve,*
> *By his loved mansionry, that the Heaven's breath*
> *Smells wooingly here. . . .*

Neher insisted on having a semi-dilapidated grey keep of striking poverty. The guests' words of praise were merely compliments.

He saw the Macbeths as petty Scottish nobility, and neurotically ambitious.

His sets are significant statements about reality. He takes a bold sweep, never letting inessential detail or decoration distract from the statement, which is an artistic and an intellectual one. At the same time everything has beauty, and the essential detail is most lovingly carried out.

With what care he selects a chair, and with what thought he places it! And it all helps the playing. One chair will have short legs, and the height of the accompanying table will also be calculated, so that whoever eats at it has to take up a quite specific attitude, and the conversation of these people as they bend more than usual when eating takes on a particular character, which makes the episode clearer. And how many effects are made possible by his doors of the most diverse heights!

This master knows every craft and is careful to see that even the poorest furniture is executed in an artistic way, for the symptoms of poverty and cheapness have to be prepared with art. So materials like iron, wood, canvas are expertly handled and properly combined, economically or lavishly as the play demands. He goes to the blacksmith's shop to have the swords forged and to the artificial florist's to get tin wreaths cut and woven. Many of the props are museum pieces.

These small objects which he puts in the actors' hands – weapons, instruments, purses, cutlery, etc. – are always authentic and will pass the closest inspection; but when it comes to architecture – i.e. when he builds interiors or exteriors – he is content to give indications, poetic and artistic representations of a hut or a locality which do honour as much to his imagination as to his power of observing. They display a lovely mixture of his own handwriting and that of the playwright. And there is no building of his, no yard or workshop or garden, that does not also bear the fingerprints, as it were, of the people who built it or who lived there. He makes visible the manual skills and knowledge of the builders and the ways of living of the inhabitants.

In his designs our friend always starts with 'the people themselves' and 'what is happening to or through them'. He provides no 'décor', frames and backgrounds, but constructs the space for 'people' to experience something in. Almost all that the stage designer's art consists in he can do standing on his head. Of course, Shakespeare's Rome was different from Racine's. He constructs the poets' stage and it glows.* If he wants he can achieve a richer effect with a varied structure of different greys and whites than many other artists with the entire palette. He is a great painter. But above all he is an ingenious story-teller. He knows better than anyone that whatever does not further the narrative harms it. Accordingly he is always content to give indications wherever something 'plays no part'. At the same time these indications are stimulating. They arouse the spectator's imagination, which perfect reproduction would numb.

He often makes use of a device which has since become an international commonplace and is generally divorced from its sense. That is the division of the stage, an arrangement by which a room, a yard or a place of work is built up to half-height downstage while another environment is projected or painted behind, changing with every scene or remaining throughout the play. This second milieu can be made up of documentary material or a picture or a tapestry. Such an arrangement naturally gives depth to the story while acting as a continual reminder to the audience that the scene designer has built a set: what he sees is presented differently from the world outside the theatre.

This method, for all its flexibility, is, of course, only one among the many he uses; his sets are as different from one another as the plays themselves. The basic impression is of very lightly constructed, easily transformed and beautiful pieces of scaffolding, which further the acting and help to tell the evening's story fluently. Add the verve with which he works, the contempt he shows for anything dainty and innocuous, and the gaiety of his constructions, and you have perhaps some indication of the way of working of the greatest stage designer of our day.

* Thanks to the poverty of our lighting arrangements, the splendour of Neher's sets cannot be photographically reproduced.

The Dramaturg's Speech about Casting

Parts are allotted wrongly and thoughtlessly. As if all cooks were fat, all peasants phlegmatic, all statesmen stately. As if all who love and are loved were beautiful. As if all good speakers had a fine voice.

Of course, there is a lot that has to be taken into account. This Mephisto and this Gretchen will go with this particular Faust. There are actors who are not easy to imagine as a prince; there are all kinds of princes, but at least they have all been brought up to command; and *Hamlet* is a prince among thousands.

Then actors must be able to develop. Here is a young man who will make a better Troilus once he has played Amtsdiener Mitteldorf.* Here we have an actress who hasn't the lasciviousness needed for Gretchen in the last act: can she get it by playing Cressida (whose situations demand it) or Grusha (whose situations rule it out completely)?

Certainly any actor is better suited to some parts than to others. And yet it may harm him to confine himself to one particular type. Only the most gifted are competent to portray characters mutually alike, twins as it were, recognizable as such and yet easily distinguished.

It is pure folly to allot parts according to physical characteristics. 'He has a kingly figure.' What does that mean? Do all kings have to look like *Edward VII*? 'But he lacks a commanding presence.' Are there so few ways of commanding? 'She seems too respectable for Mother Courage.' Have a look at the fishwives.

Can one go by temperament? One can't. That again would be taking the easy way out.

True, there are gentle people and noisy, violent ones. But it is also true that every man has every variety of temperament. And the more of an actor he happens to be, the truer that is. And those varieties which he is repressing may be particularly effective when brought out. Parts, moreover, which are conceived on a big scale

* (Trans.) In *Biberpelz und Roter Hahn*, an adaptation from Hauptmann.

(even small ones) not only show strongly marked features but have room for additions; they are like maps with blank patches. The actor must cultivate all varieties of temperament, for his characters only come to life by means of their own contradictoriness. It is most dangerous to cast a major part on the strength of a single characteristic.

FRAGMENTS FROM THE FOURTH NIGHT

Cheerful Criticism

THE ACTOR: One can understand people getting pleasure from sharing the characters' emotions and spiritually participating in their actions. But how are they supposed to get pleasure from criticizing these things?

THE PHILOSOPHER: I've often found myself being depressed by taking part in your various heroes' actions, and generally disgusted by having to share their emotions. On the other hand, I like playing around with your heroes; that's to say, it entertains me to imagine different ways of behaving and compare their actions with others that are equally possible.

THE DRAMATURG: But how else can they behave, being what they are, and designed for what they are designed for? How can you conceive a different way of behaving for them?

THE PHILOSOPHER: I can do it. And I can compare them with myself too, for that matter.

THE DRAMATURG: So exercising one's critical faculties isn't a purely intellectual business?

THE PHILOSOPHER: Of course not. You can't possibly confine criticism to the intellect. Feelings also play a part in the process, and it may be your particular job to organize criticism by means of feelings. Remember that criticism originates in crisis and reinforces it.

THE DRAMATURG: I agree we need to know as much as possible in order to stage even the smallest scene. Then what?

THE PHILOSOPHER: Degrees of knowledge vary widely. There's knowledge in your dreams and premonitions, in your hopes and cares, in liking and in suspicion. But above all knowledge manifests itself in knowing better, i.e. in contradiction. There's your territory for you.

THE ACTOR: It's all got to be shown-to-the-children, in other words. There's nothing audiences loathe more than being sent back to school.

THE PHILOSOPHER: Your schools must have been terrible ones to inspire such loathing. But why should I bother about your bad schools? Get rid of them!

THE DRAMATURG: Nobody objects to a play having a meaning, but it mustn't be continually thrust at you. The lesson has got to be unobtrusive.

THE PHILOSOPHER: Believe me: people who want unobtrusive lessons want no lessons at all. As for the meaning being thrust at you, that's another matter.

THE DRAMATURG: Well, we've done our best to study your various dispositions for making the art of the theatre just as instructive as science. You invited us to come and work in your thaëter, which was supposed to be a scientific institute; making art was not supposed to be our object. To achieve what you want, however, we've had to throw in our entire art. Frankly, if we are to act as you wish and with the aims you wish, we shall be creating art just the same.

THE PHILOSOPHER: That has occurred to me too.

THE DRAMATURG: You've scrapped so much of what's normally supposed to be needed for the exercise of art, yet it strikes me that what counted was your retention of one single point.

THE PHILOSOPHER: What?

THE DRAMATURG: What you called the ease of this work. The

realization that this game of preference, this cooking things up for the audience, can only be conducted in a cheerful, good-tempered mood, a mood where one's disposed for fun. You placed art just right when you pointed out the difference between the work of a man who's responsible for pushing five buttons on a machine and a man who juggles with five balls. And you linked this ease with extreme seriousness in one's attitude to one's social task.

THE ACTOR: What most put me off at the beginning was your insistence on working purely and solely with the reason. Thinking is such a thin-blooded business, you see; it's fundamentally inhuman. Even if you argued that it was the distinguishing mark of the human animal it'd be a mistake, because I'd say you were leaving out the animal part.

THE PHILOSOPHER: How do you feel now?

THE ACTOR: Oh, I've come to think thinking isn't so cold-blooded after all. There's no contradiction with feeling. And what I stimulate in the audience isn't only thoughts but feelings. I now see thinking just as a way of behaving, and behaving socially at that. It's something that the whole body takes part in, with all its senses.

THE PHILOSOPHER: I once saw a Russian play in which workers gave a gun to a violent criminal so that he could protect them against violence while they worked. The audience simultaneously wept and laughed at this. In the old-fashioned theatre the hero used to be contrasted with a stock figure. Caricature is the means by which the empathetic kind of representation expresses criticism. The actor is criticizing life, and the spectator identifies himself with his criticisms. Probably the epic theatre can only stage such caricatures when what it wants to show is the process of caricaturing. The caricatures then make their appearance like dancers in a masked ball scene. The gliding, flitting, transitory (but not transporting) method of representation is furthermore needed because every utterance of every character has got to be made striking, and this means that the course, connexion, development of all these utterances has got to be made striking too. Genuine understanding and criticism are only possible if the part and the whole and the varying relations between the part and the whole can all be understood and criticized. People's utterances are bound to be contradictory, so we are bound to take in the whole contradiction. The actor doesn't need to put forward a fully elaborated character. He couldn't do it, and he doesn't have to. He's not only putting forward criticism of the matter in hand, but first and foremost the matter itself. He doesn't need to have fully worked-out opinions about everything he puts forward. He is **drawing on** a pool of things seen and experienced.

THE ACTOR: All the same, our theatre is a serious obstacle to your thaëter, my friend. Take those abilities of ours which the theatre has developed for its own ends; their utilization is going to suffer from the fact that certain of our capacities are of little use to you, as well as those which you actually need. It's just as much of a handicap that they should in some ways exceed your requirements as that they should fall short.

THE PHILOSOPHER: When do they exceed them?

THE ACTOR: You explained very clearly the difference between someone who *sees* and someone who *looks critically*. You suggested that the former must be replaced by the latter. Down with guessing, hurrah for knowing! Down with suspicion, hurrah for conviction! Down with feelings, hurrah for argument! Down with dreams, hurrah for plans! Down with yearning, hurrah for determination!

The Actress applauds him.

THE ACTOR: Well, why aren't you applauding?

THE PHILOSOPHER: I wasn't really being so definite about art's broad tasks. Certainly I was against the contrary attitude: Down with knowing, hurrah for guessing, and so on. I opposed the idea of keeping art as something strictly marginal. Slogans like these don't apply to the works of progressive classes and stirring times. But look at our own period. Look what much more artistic performances you get from works based on the attitudes I'm against. Guessing is far more artistically portrayed than knowing. Even where works do include clear ideas it's on their unclear side that one finds the artistic element. I don't just mean that one looks for it there, but that one actually finds it.

THE DRAMATURG: You don't think there's an artistic form for knowing?

THE PHILOSOPHER: I'm afraid not. Why should I want to knock out the whole realm of guessing, dreaming and feeling? People do tackle social problems in these ways. Guessing and knowledge aren't opposites. Guessing can lead to knowledge, knowledge to guessing. Dreams can lead to plans, plans can merge into dreams. I yearn for something and set out, and I still yearn as I move. One thinks feelings and one feels thoughtfully. But there are also short cuts and short circuits. There are stages where dreams don't turn into plans, guessing doesn't turn into knowledge, yearning doesn't get on the move. Those are bad periods for art; it becomes bad. The tension between guessing and knowledge, from which art arises, snaps. The field as it were loses its charge. At the moment I am not so much interested in what comes of those artists who are plunged in mysticism. I'm more interested in those who turn impatiently away from planless dreaming and go on to a dreamless planning, to a corresponding empty plan.

THE DRAMATURG: I see. It is specifically we who are trying to serve the society that we belong to, who have to measure all the dimensions of *every* sphere of human activity.

THE ACTOR: So we're not just to show what we know?

THE ACTRESS: Also what we guess.

THE PHILOSOPHER: Remember that some things you don't know may be recognized by the audience.

THE ACTOR: Did the Augsburger say anything about his audience?

THE PHILOSOPHER: Yes. This:

The other day I met my audience.
In a dusty street
He gripped a pneumatic drill in his fists.

For a second
He looked up. Rapidly I set up my theatre
Between the houses. He
Looked expectant.

In the pub
I met him again. He was standing at the bar.
Grimy with sweat, he was drinking. In his fist
A thick sandwich. Rapidly I set up my theatre. He
looked astonished.

Today
I brought it off again. Outside the station
With brass bands and rifle butts I saw him
Being herded off to war.
In the midst of the crowd
I set up my theatre. Over his shoulder
He looked back
And nodded.

THE PHILOSOPHER: The workers' opponents aren't a unified reactionary mass. Nor is the individual member of the opposing classes a unified, packaged and guaranteed hundred-per-cent hostile body. The class struggle has infected his own inner self. He is torn apart by his interests. Living as one of the mass he is bound to share the mass's interests, however isolated his life. In the Soviet film *The Battleship Potemkin* there were even some bourgeois who joined in the workers' applause when the sailors threw their officer persecutors overboard. Although this bourgeoisie had been protected from the social revolution by its officers it had never managed to assimilate them. It was always frightened of (and experiencing) infringements of its own authority. So bourgeois and proletarians occasionally joined together to vote against feudalism. And this meant that these bourgeois came at such moments into genuine and enjoyable contact with the progressive proletarian elements in human society; they felt themselves to be part of humanity as a whole, solving questions in a large-scale and powerful manner. It shows that art can create a certain unity in its audience, which in our period is divided into classes.

THE PHILOSOPHER: However much of what's considered essential to the art of the theatre we may wish to abandon for the sake of our new aims, there is one thing which we must, in my view, preserve at all costs, and that's its quality of ease.* It can't be any handicap to us, and if we gave it up it would mean straining and spoiling our resources. There is something naturally light and easy about the theatre. This business of making up one's face and adopting rehearsed positions, this imitation of the world with so little to go on, this giving some notion of life, these epigrams and abbreviations – the whole thing has got to retain its natural cheerfulness if it isn't to be just silly. You can achieve any amount of seriousness within such ease, none at all without it. So when we put a problem in a form which allows it to be raised in a play we must do so in a playful manner. We're working with a very fine balance, making calculated movements, elegantly, without caring how the ground is crumbling under our feet. People might indeed object to our sitting here between bloody wars discussing, without any thought of escapism, the sort of theatrical matters that seem to owe their existence to men's need for distraction. Tomorrow all of us may go up in smoke. But we are concentrating on the theatre precisely because we wish to prepare a means of pursuing our affairs via the theatre too. We must not be led by the urgency of our situation to destroy the means we want to make use of. The more haste, the less speed. The surgeon who has heavy responsibilities needs the little scalpel to lie lightly and easily in his hand. The world is out of joint, certainly, and it will take powerful movements to manipulate it all back again. But among the various relevant instruments there can be one that is slight and delicate and needs to be handled with ease.

* (Trans.) *Leichtigkeit* means both ease and lightness, an ambiguity impossible to convey in one English word.

THE PHILOSOPHER: A theatre that can't be laughed in is a theatre to be laughed at. Humourless people are ridiculous. Sometimes it is hoped that ceremonious presentation will give things a meaning they otherwise lack. When things have a meaning then sufficient ceremony will be generated if that meaning is brought out. The photographs of the crowds at Lenin's funeral show that something ceremonious is going on. At first all you see is people still trying to accompany a man whom they don't want to let go. But there are a great many of them, and moreover they are 'insignificant' people and by their accompanying this man they are demonstrating against a certain minority who had long worked to be rid of him. Cares like that absolve one from caring about ceremony.

Definition of Art

THE PHILOSOPHER: We've talked enough about the uses art can be put to, about how it can be created and what the creation of art depends on, and we have also created art during these four nights; so we can now risk a few cautious statements of an abstract kind about this peculiar human capacity, trusting that they won't be applied abstractly, independently and purely on their own. Thus we might perhaps say that art is skill in preparing reproductions of human beings' life together such as lead people to a particular kind of feeling, thought and action that would not be stimulated in the same way or to the same extent by seeing or experiencing the reality reproduced. Out of his own seeing and experiencing of reality the artist has made a picture that reproduces his thoughts and feelings and is for us to see and experience.

THE DRAMATURG: There's a good phrase for that in German: 'der Künstler produziert sich.' – in other words, the artist doesn't just express himself but produces himself.

THE PHILOSOPHER: It's a good phrase if you take it to mean that in the artist man is producing himself: that it's art when man produces himself.

THE ACTOR: But that can't possibly be all that art can do, because it just wouldn't be enough. What about the dreams dreamt by dreamers, beauty with an admixture of terror, life on all its different levels?

THE DRAMATURG: Yes, it's about time we talked about enjoyment. You may think the whole of philosophy lies in making life more enjoyable, but you seem to want art to be of such a sort that it of all things cannot be enjoyed. Eating a good dish you estimate highly; fobbing the people off with potatoes you condemn. But art is to have nothing in common with eating and drinking or love.

THE PHILOSOPHER: Thus art is a peculiar and fundamental human capacity: not a disguise for morality or a prettification of knowledge but an independent discipline that represents the various other disciplines in a contradictory manner. To describe art as the ream of the beautiful is to set about it in too passive and all-embracing a way. Artists deploy skill: that is the first point. What makes artificial things beautiful is the fact of their being skilfully made. You may complain that mere skill isn't enough for the creation of art objects, but the expression 'mere' can only refer to a hollow, one-sided kind of skill which is based on a single artistic field and is lacking from all others: i.e. which is unskilful on the moral and scientific side. Beauty in nature is a quality which gives the human senses a chance to be skilful. The eye is producing itself. That isn't an independent process which stops there. Nor is it one that has not been prepared by other processes, social processes, processes involving other types of production. Where would the mountain's vast sweep be without the constriction of the valley, or the informal form of the wilderness without the formal formlessness of the great cities? No man's eye can be sated if he is not sated himself. Pitched into it without any possibility of making use of it, anybody who is exhausted or got there accidentally finds that even the most 'fabulous' of beauty spots just has a depressing effect on him; it is the impossibility of any such possibility that is depressing. Untrained people often feel beauty's impact when contrasts grow sharper: when the blue water becomes bluer, the red sunset redder, the golden corn more golden.

THE PHILOSOPHER: From the point of view of art we can say that our progress has been as follows. We have taken those imitations of reality which release all sorts of emotions and passions and tried to improve them without bothering about the latter by arranging them in such a manner that anyone seeing them is put in a position actively to master the reality imitated. We have found that more accurate imitations lead to the release of emotions and passions: in fact, that emotions and passions can further the mastering of reality.

THE DRAMATURG: There's really no longer anything surprising in the fact that art was almost ruined at first by applying it to a new business – that of destroying men's preconceptions about their life together in society. Nowadays we can see that this happened because art tackled that new business without abandoning one of its preconceptions about itself. Its entire apparatus was designed for the business of making men accept their fate. The apparatus was ruined when the part of man's fate in its productions was suddenly taken by man himself. In short, it wanted to promote the new business while remaining the old art. Accordingly it did everything in a hesitant, half-hearted, selfish, conscience-ridden way; but nothing suits art worse than this. It was only by sacrificing itself that it became itself again.

THE ACTOR: I see: what seemed inartistic was what didn't suit the old art, not what didn't suit art in general.

THE PHILOSOPHER: That's why some people, on seeing the new art so apparently feeble – or rather, enfeebled: enfeebled by its new tasks without those tasks having been satisfactorily solved – regretfully turned their backs and preferred to give the new tasks up.

THE ACTOR: This whole notion of practicable definitions strikes me as a bit cold and austere. We'll merely be producing solutions to problems.

THE DRAMATURG: Unsolved problems too, mind you.

THE ACTOR: Yes, but in order to get them solved. That's not life any more. People may choose to see it as a network of solved – or unsolved – problems, but problems aren't the whole of life. Life has its unproblematic side too, and there are also such things as insoluble problems. I don't want to be restricted to playing charades.

THE DRAMATURG: I can understand him. He wants to 'dig deep'. A mixture of the expected and the unexpected, the intelligible and the unintelligible. He wants to mix applause with terror, amusement with regret. In short, he wishes to make art.

THE ACTOR: I can't stand all that talk about art being the handmaiden of society. There sits society, fat and powerful. Art isn't a part of her; it just belongs to her; it's simply her skivvy. Are we all supposed to be a lot of servants? Can't we all be masters? Can't art become a mistress? Let's get rid of domestic service altogether, in art just as much as anywhere else!

THE PHILOSOPHER: Bravo!

THE DRAMATURG: What d'you mean, bravo? You've ruined everything you've said by that piece of spontaneous applause. All anybody has to do is tell you he's oppressed and you're on his side at once.

THE PHILOSOPHER: I hope I am. I see what he's getting at now. He's worried we're going to turn him into a Civil Servant or a a master of ceremonies or a revivalist preacher operating by 'artistic means'. Cheer up; that's not the plan. The art of acting needs to be treated simply as an elementary human utterance which contains its own purpose. That's where it differs from the art of war, whose purpose is external to itself. The art of acting is one of society's elementary capacities; it is based on a direct social asset, one of humanity's pleasures in society; it is like language itself; it's really a language of its own. I propose we rise to our feet to make this tribute stick in our memory.
All rise.

And now I propose that we should take advantage of the fact that we've risen to our feet, and go and relieve ourselves.

THE ACTOR: Oh God, you've wrecked the whole thing. I protest.

THE PHILOSOPHER: Why? Once again I'm obeying an instinct, bowing to it, respecting it, and at the same time seeing that the ceremony comes to a suitably banal conclusion.

There is a pause.

The Audience of Statesmen

THE PHILOSOPHER: We have seen that our thaëter will be extremely different from that famous, universal, well-tested and indispensable institution, the theatre. One important difference which may comfort you is the fact that it is not supposed to be thrown open for all eternity. It is meant only for our own day, precisely for our own day: which admittedly isn't a cheerful one.

THE PHILOSOPHER: It has to come out; I can't conceal it from you any longer. I've no equipment, no building, no theatre, not a single costume, not even a pot of make-up. I'm backed by nobody and nothing. Your efforts will have to be greater than any you've made so far, but there is going to be no money for them, and we can't even ask you to do it for the glory. For we can't provide glory either. No newspapers ever glorified our collaborators.

Pause.

THE ACTOR: So all you would be asking for would be work for work's sake.

THE WORKER: That's a rotten think to ask. I'd never ask anybody that; I've heard it too often. 'Don't you enjoy the work itself?' they say in a disappointed voice when I put in for my wages. 'Don't you work for the sake of the work?' No, whatever happens we're going to pay. Not much, because we haven't got much, but not nothing, because work has got to be paid for.

THE DRAMATURG: I think you've more chance of getting artists by giving them nothing than offering them a pittance. If they're playing for nothing, then at least they are giving.

THE ACTOR: You people would pay a pittance, would you? All right, I'd accept it. By all means. It puts some sense into our relationship and makes an ordinary workaday affair of it. One doesn't look a gift horse in the mouth, and this is supposed, after all, to be an art whose mouth one can inspect. I've understood that much: here's a horse who really wants his mouth to be looked at. That settles the financial side, more or less.

THE DRAMATURG: It's lucky for you that artists are so frivolous, I'd say. It's quite slipped his mind that he's got to give up transforming himself into a king every evening.

THE ACTOR: Against that it seems that in this new theatre I shall be free to transform my audience into kings. Not only into the semblance of kings, but into the real thing. Into statesmen, thinkers and engineers. What an audience I'll have! What goes on in the world I shall bring before their judgement seat. And what a distinguished, useful and celebrated place my theatre will be if it is to become a laboratory for this great mass of working people. I too shall act according to the classic principle: Alter the world; it needs it.

THE WORKER: It sounds a bit pretentious. But why shouldn't it? It stands for a great cause.

Appendices to the Messingkauf Theory

First Appendix to the Messingkauf Theory

The theory is relatively simple. It deals with the traffic between stage and auditorium: how the spectator must master the incidents on the stage. The theatrical experience comes about by means of an act of empathy; this is established in Aristotle's *Poetics*. The critical attitude cannot be among the elements that go to make it up, so defined; the better the empathy works, the truer this must be. Criticism is stimulated with reference to the way empathy is generated, not with reference to the incidents that the spectator sees reproduced on the stage. Not that it is entirely proper to speak of 'incidents that the spectator sees reproduced on the stage' when talking about the Aristotelian theatre. Story and performance in the Aristotelian theatre are not meant to provide reproductions of incidents in real life, but to bring about the whole theatrical experience as laid down (complete with certain cathartic effects). Admittedly there is a need for actions recalling real life, and they have to have a certain element of probability to create the illusions without which empathy cannot take place. But there is no need for the causality of the incidents to be brought out; it is enough that it should not give rise to scepticism.* It is only the man who is mainly concerned with those real-life incidents on which the theatre bases its playing who finds himself able to treat the incidents on the stage as reproductions of reality and to criticize them as such. In doing so he is stepping out of the realm of art, for art does not see its primary task as the mere provision of reproductions. Once again: it is

* It is theoretically possible to bring about a complete theatrical experience by totally misrepresenting an incident from real life.

concerned only with quite specific reproductions, that is to say reproductions with specific effects. The act of empathy that produces them would only be thrown out of gear if the spectator were to go into the actual incidents critically. So the question is this: is it quite impossible to make the reproduction of real-life incidents the purpose of art and thereby make something conducive to art of the spectators' critical attitude towards them? As soon as one starts to go into this it becomes clear that so great a transformation could only be brought about by changing the nature of the traffic between auditorium and stage. In this new method of practising art empathy would lose its dominant role. Against that the Alienation effect (A-effect) will need to be introduced, which is an artistic effect too and also leads to a theatrical experience. It consists in the reproduction of real-life incidents on the stage in such a way as to underline their causality and bring it to the spectator's attention. This type of art also generates emotions; such performances facilitate the mastering of reality; and this it is that moves the spectator. The A-effect is an ancient artistic technique; it is known from classical comedy, certain branches of popular art and the practices of the Asiatic theatre.

Second Appendix to the Messingkauf Theory

A few points will serve to show what part dialectical materialism plays in the theory:

I

The *self-evident* – i.e. the particular shape our consciousness gives our experience – is resolved into its components when counteracted by the A-effect and turned into a new form of the *evident*. An imposed schema is being broken up here. The individual's own experiences correct or confirm what he has taken over from the community. The original act of discovery is repeated.

2

The contradiction between empathy and detachment is made stronger and becomes an element in the performance.

3

Historicizing involves judging a particular social system from another social system's point of view. The standpoints in question result from the development of society. Note: Aristotelian dramaturgy takes no account (i.e. allows none to be taken) of the objective contradictions in any process. They have to be changed into subjective ones, located in the hero.

Third Appendix to the Messingkauf Theory

The spectator's need nowadays to be distracted from his daily warfare is continually reproduced by that daily warfare, but just as continually in conflict with his need to be able to control his own fate. Among such needs an artificial distinction is made between entertainment and maintenance; entertainment (of a distracting kind) is a continual threat to maintenance, since the spectator isn't led into the void – not into an unfamiliar world, but into a distorted one – and he pays for his extravagances, which he regards as mere excursions, in real life. Identifying himself with his enemy does not leave him unmarked; it makes him an enemy to himself. Surrogates satisfy one's need and poison one's body; the audience want both to be diverted and to be converted – and they must want to be both – from the daily warfare.

The new theatre is simply a theatre of the man who has begun to help himself. In three hundred years of organization and technology he has been transformed. The theatre has been very slow to come of age. Shakespearian man is helplessly handed over to his fate, i.e. to his passions. Society holds out no hand to him. There is a quite limited radius within which a given type's splendour and vitality is effective.

The new theatre appeals to social man because man has helped himself in a social way technically, scientifically and politically. It exposes any given type together with his way of behaving, so as to throw light on his social motivations; he can only be grasped if they are mastered. Individuals remain individual, but become a social phenomenon; their passions and also their fates become a social concern. The individual's position in society loses its God-given quality and becomes the centre of attention. The A-effect is a social measure.

Fourth Appendix to the Messingkauf Theory

I

Under the Aristotelian system of constructing a play and the style of acting that goes with it (the two concepts can be switched round if you like) the audience's deception with regard to the way in which the incidents shown on the stage come about and take place in real life is helped by the fact that the story's presentation forms an indivisible whole. Its details cannot be compared one by one with their corresponding parts in real life. Nothing must be taken 'out of its context' in order, say, to set it in the context of reality. The answer lies in the alienating style of acting. In this the story line is a broken one; the single whole is made up of independent parts which can and must be compared with the corresponding part-incidents in real life. This way of acting draws all its force from comparisons with reality; in other words, it is continually drawing attention to the causality of the incidents reproduced.

2

To achieve the A-effect the actor must give up his *complete conversion* into the stage character. He *shows* the character, he *quotes* his lines, he *repeats* a real-life incident. The audience is not entirely 'carried away'; it need not conform psychologically, adopt a fatalistic attitude towards fate as portrayed. (It can feel anger where the character feels joy, and so on. It is free, and sometimes even encouraged, to imagine a different course of events or to try and find one, and so forth.) The incidents are *historicized* and socially *set*. (The former, of course, occurs above all with present-day incidents: whatever is was not always, and will not always be so. The latter repeatedly casts a questionable light on the prevailing social order and subjects it to discussion.) Achieving the A-effect is a technique that has to be taught from first principles.

3

One establishes laws by accepting natural incidents with astonishment, as it were; in other words, one can only understand their evidence by ceasing to treat them as 'self-evident'. In order to discover the law governing falling bodies alternative possibilities must be imagined for them; among these imagined possibilities the actual, natural possibility will then be the right one, and the imagined alternatives will emerge as impossibilities. The theatre can stimulate the audience to this astounded, inventive and critical attitude by means of its A-effect, but the fact that this is an attitude that also has to be adopted in the sciences by no means makes a scientific institution of it. It is merely a theatre of the scientific age. It takes the attitude adopted by its audience in real life and applies it to the theatrical experience. Or, to put it another way: empathy is not the sole source of emotions at art's disposal.

4

Within the conventions of the Aristotelian theatre the kind of acting we described above would be a mere matter of style. It is much more. All the same, there is no question of the theatre thereby losing its old functions of entertainment and instruction; these actually get a new lease of life. The method of representation becomes wholly natural once more. It can display the various different styles. Concern with reality sets the imagination off on the right pleasurable road. Gaiety and seriousness revive in criticism, which is of a creative kind. Altogether it is a matter of taking the old religious institution and secularizing it.

Notes

A note of Brecht's early in 1939 says that he has been writing 'a lot of theory in dialogue form'. Another, at the end of 1942, that he is still working on the 'Messingkauf'. The dialogues collected in the present volume were written during those four years. He noted that he had been prompted to adopt this form by the Dialogues of Galileo Galilei, which he had studied when working on his play about the great physicist's life. Dialogue form was nothing new in his theoretical writings, however: he had used it on a number of occasions in the twenties for discussions of acting. It allowed a subject to be approached from several points of view, and ideas to emerge from a conflict of opinions.

Brecht wrote the 'Messingkauf' dialogues in four distinct versions. Apart from one almost complete conversation, all the manuscripts remained fragmentary. He never managed to combine the various scraps together as he had intended. When in 1948 he called the 'Short Organum for the Theatre' a 'condensation of the Messingkauf' this was true only of the kernel of the dialogues. In point of fact the 'Messingkauf' and the 'Short Organum' interestingly complement one another. In the dialogues the invasion of the theatre by philosophy is still under discussion; by the time of the 'Short Organum' it is the presupposition on which the structure rests.

Brecht had various plans for the 'Messingkauf' conversations. About the general idea of this project he wrote: 'The philosopher insists on the P (for "planetarium") rather than R (for "roundabout") type: a theatre for purely didactic purposes, which simply models people's movements (including psychological movements) so that they can be studied, showing the workings of social relationships in such a way that society can intervene. His wishes are resolved in the theatre, the theatre putting them into effect. Criticism of the theatre leads to a new theatre. The whole thrown open to learning, with exercises and experiments. In the centre, the A-effect.'

This 'four-sided conversation about a new way of making theatre', as Brecht subsequently described it in *Theaterarbeit*, was divided into four Nights (unlike the *Decameron*, with its division into Days). The first collection of material he made proposes the following arrangement:

> *First night:* The Philosopher is welcomed to the theatre/ business is good/the escape from reality to the theatre/there's old theatre and new/competition from the cinema/cinema, a test of gestics/literarization/montage/reality/capitalism, the poker-faced man/reality in the theatre/the Philosopher's requirements/the appeal/commitment.

> *Second night:* Aristotle's *Poetics*/the emotion racket/the new subject-matter/the hero/R type and P type/Fascist theatricals/ science/foundation of the thaëter.

> *Third night:* The street scene/the A-effect/the smokers' theatre/exercises/fear and misery/variations on Shakespeare.

> *Fourth night:* Reconversion to a theatre/Chaplin/comedy/ fairground narrative/Chinese acting/cheerful criticism.

The topics outlined in this plan are only partly dealt with in the fragments. In none of the four collections, for instance, are such themes as 'cinema, a test of gestics', 'Fascist theatricals', 'comedy', and 'fairground narrative' worked out. Nor are there any dialogues about 'R type and P type', though they occur a number of times in the plans. This and further subjects intended for treatment in the 'Messingkauf' are discussed in an essay* which Brecht wrote in another connexion.

* (Ed.) Brecht used the term 'Roundabout type' to describe those who identify themselves with an incident, like a child on a roundabout; the 'Planetarium types' are those who are confronted with a demonstration and observe it, like the spectators in a planetarium. See 'K-Typus und P-Typus' in *Schriften zum Theater* 5, pp. 60 ff. (not yet translated into English).

In the remaining three collections of material Brecht allocated some of these topics to different nights. The arrangement changed a number of times in course of writing.

The 'Messingkauf' dialogues are arranged to correspond with the rather more extensive selection in *Schriften zum Theater 5*. The present volume collects the dialogues but omits the essays and the 'Messingkauf' poems ('Poems on the Theatre') which go beyond the original plan of a four-sided conversation. The arrangement of the fragments is intended to follow Brecht's scheme as closely as possible. In selecting and compiling them the editor has departed from the plan where Brecht failed to carry it out. Thus the original idea was for the Fourth Night to provide a kind of 'solution' of the problems raised. Brecht commented: 'On the aesthetic plane (which must not in any way be treated as "higher" than the doctrinaire plane) the problem of didacticism becomes an absolute aesthetic problem which is resolved as it were autarchically. Utilitarianism is here made to disappear in an unusual way, cropping up only in the saying "what's useful is beautiful". Practicable images of reality correspond simply to our period's sense of beauty. The poets' "dreams" are merely addressed to a new audience, whose relations with practical activity are not the same as before: the poets themselves are men of this period. This is the dialectical twist in the Fourth Night of the "Messingkauf". The Philosopher's plan to apply art to didactic ends is absorbed in the artists' plan to put their knowledge, their experience and their social problems into their art.' A solution in this sense was not possible given the material available.

It was not easy to fit the 'Messingkauf' fragments together. The intention was to make the 'seams' or junction points left by the editor visible at all costs. These seams are indicated by the spaces between fragments. Titles in square brackets are not Brecht's own. The rest are taken from his dispositions.

The volume ends with the 'Appendices to the Messingkauf Theory' which Brecht noted down while working on the dialogues. They provide a theoretical résumé and it is difficult to understand this great torso without them.

The First Night

This is the section for which there are most notes and sketches. In the opening dialogue (pp. 11–21) Brecht has carried out one of his plans. It is in effect the only dialogue that represents his conception of a 'Night', even though it omits the introductory 'The Philosopher is welcomed to the theatre' and the final 'The Philosopher salutes the theatre'.

p. 21. *Naturalism.* The text 'Naturalism didn't last very long' (p. 25) is headed by Brecht 'Naturalism – Realism'.

p. 27. *Empathy.* The text 'Mime suddenly started flourishing' (p. 28) was not originally attributed to a speaker. It has been given to the Dramaturg as being the expert on theatrical history and forms.

p. 30. *About ignorance.* The title 'From the Philosopher's Speech about the Ignorance of the Majority' applies in the original only to the first section (and there reads 'the Visitor's', not 'The Philosopher's'), but the editor has added further fragments relating to the same theme. The texts 'It's because people know so little', 'Because people nowadays' and 'The ancients thought' (p. 31) were headed by Brecht 'From the Philosopher's Speech about Ignorance'.

The Second Night

p. 43. *The Actor's Speech about how to Portray a Little Nazi.* Brecht specified no particular night for this.

p. 44. *Science.* The text 'People who know nothing about either' was intended for the Fourth Night. It has here been transposed and given to the Philosopher because it belongs thematically with this section. The dialogues 'You allot a very important place' (p. 50) and 'Surely you're not telling me' (p. 55) have no particular night specified for them.

p. 51. *Removal of Illusion and Empathy.* The first dialogue was intended for the Third Night. The Philosopher's remarks starting 'What kind of thinking are we talking about?' are headed 'Thinking'.

p. 57. Shakespeare's Theatre. These texts were mainly intended for this Night, though part was meant for the Fourth Night. The dialogue 'What about Tragedy in Shakespeare?' (p. 59) is headed 'Tragedy in Shakespeare'.

p. 64. Piscator's Theatre. The first text is headed 'From the description of Piscator's theatre on the Second Night'; the second, 'Piscator's Theatre'.

The Third Night

p. 68. The Augsburger's Theatre. These dialogues and descriptions are labelled partly for the Third Night, partly for the Fourth. The opening text ('Piscator was making') is headed 'The Playwright's relation to Piscator'; it is not allotted to any specific night. The section starting 'He was a young man . . .' (p. 69) is headed 'The Augsburger'. A subsequent note in Brecht's handwriting says that the term 'The Augsburger', which is used with almost complete consistency all through the 'Messingkauf', should be replaced throughout by 'the playwright'. (See translator's footnote, p. 67.) The text 'The Augsburger's theatre was very small' (p. 70) bears the same heading.

p. 76. The A-effect. The opening section 'If empathy makes . . .' was intended for the Second Night. The texts 'The main reason why . . .' (p. 76), 'Doesn't the surrealist movement . . .' (p. 77), and 'It's one of the greatest achievements . . .' (p. 81) are allotted to no particular night. The rest are intended for the Third Night.

The Fourth Night

p. 84. The Playwright's Speech . . . Neither this speech nor the 'Dramaturg's Speech about Casting' (p. 87) were included in the early manuscripts. Both were first published in *Theaterarbeit* in 1952.

p. 88. Cheerful criticism. The dialogue starting 'It's all got to be shown-to-the-children' was intended for the Second Night. 'The workers' opponents . . .' (p. 93) and 'However much . . .' (p. 94) (originally headed 'On Ease') are not allotted to any particular night.

p. 95. *Definition of Art*. This is the heading Brecht gave to the first section; the editor has added the remainder. The section starting 'This whole notion of practicable definitions' (p. 97) is allotted to no specific night.

p. 99. *The Audience of Statesmen*. Brecht's plans show that the 'Messingkauf' was to conclude with this section. The opening text (p. 99), headed 'The Theatre,' is allotted to no specific night.

Appendices to the Messingkauf Theory

Brecht wrote these on 2 and 3 August, 1940.

For its third 'Brecht-Abend' the Berliner Ensemble performed a stage version of some of the 'Messingkauf' dialogues. The première was on 12 October 1963. The dialogues were interspersed with scenes from *Arturo Ui*, *Die Mutter*, *Mother Courage*; also with the practice scenes 'Der Streit der Fischweiber' and 'Der Wettkampf des Homer und Hesiod', and with other actors' exercises based on suggestions by Brecht.

W.H.

Translator's Note

The practice scenes ('Der Mord in Pförtnerhaus', 'Der Streit der Fischweiber', 'Fährenszene' and 'Die Bedienten', together with the 'Rundgedicht' and 'Der Wettkampf des Homer und Hesiod' i.e. pp. 139–64 of *Dialoge aus dem Messingkauf*) have been omitted, as they are not part of the dialogues and no reference is made to them there. Two paragraphs referring to them in the editor's notes have correspondingly been cut. Otherwise there are no intentional changes from the German text apart from the return to the original term 'The Augsburger' on p. 67.

A note on the translator's own preliminary reading of the manuscripts, written before the present edition was made, can be found in *Brecht on Theatre* (Methuen, London, and Hill and Wang, New York, 1964), pp. 169–75. The same volume includes the 'Short Organum' mentioned above.

J.W.